LOBBYIST FOR THE PEOPLE

LOBBYIST

FOR THE

PEOPLE

A Record of Fifty Years

BENJAMIN C. MARSH

PUBLIC AFFAIRS PRESS
WASHINGTON, D. C.

58-5-32

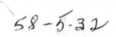

Contents

Introduction

For thirty-odd years, Ben Marsh thundered on Capitol Hill against those who sought to perpetuate and amplify economic injustices. His voice was not heard in Washington alone; his audience was America. The People's Lobby (which despite his repeated denials was in essence Ben Marsh) scattered timely and effective leaflets, reprints and bulletins across the nation. Energetic Ben often accompanied his messages in person. He escaped Washington as frequently as possible in order the better to understand and interpret the United States.

Ben Marsh was a misplaced missionary of unchallenged integrity, who came of age in the latter days of the single tax movement. He shared the energy and enthusiasm of the muckrakers. Yet an essential difference kept him from being one of them. While they concentrated upon specific reforms and specific condemnations, Ben was concerned with a pattern of basic economic change which had much in common with British Fabianism. Indeed, through frequent European trips and through wide reading he attained an acquaintance with the sweep of international social reform. Across his desk flowed an ever-expanding flood of books and pamphlets. His office became a study in disorder.

In numerous ways Ben showed himself a master at economy. Thus he was able, on a budget of $10,000 a year, to maintain an office and to publish the monthly organ, the *People's Lobby Bulletin,* as well as a miscellany of literature, tailored to meet the pressing issues of the day. One recalls a series of a half-dozen unkempt offices adjacent to the Capitol or in downtown Washington. Somehow Ben had the unfortunate knack of locating the People's Lobby in a structure about to be demolished. And yet he always turned up with new quarters, inevitably at low rental and barely large enough to crowd in his well-worn furniture and his overworked mimeograph machine. His tastes were frugal. When traveling, he stayed at the simplest hotels. His own letters to friends were frequently scrawled in longhand on the back of promotional sheets which had been mailed to him. Numerous conferences were run at a fraction of the cost of those held under the auspices of other organizations. Through personal contacts he secured free radio time. Sometimes, after having speeches inserted in the *Congressional Record,* he was able to mail them out at nominal cost. His mimeographed releases, frequently carried on his rounds in his back pocket, were scattered broadcast as he went.

Ben's ideas were so unorthodox and so challenging that in the early years of our acquaintance I tended to disagree immediately and violently with many of his notions. Like many others, however, I came to appreciate his uncanny knack of conceiving an idea many months before its validity became obvious and others took it up.

In the current parlance, he was an "inner-directed" person who always acted in accordance with basic principles. He offered tolerant but telling criticism of the programs of labor and farm movements as well as those of business. Indeed, his strictures were frequently more caustic against groups with which he was basically in sympathy than against organizations clearly dedicated to the enhancement of a selfish interest. Ben could at least understand the latter; he could not leave unchallenged the growth of selfishness, or any departure from principle, in groups which had come to strength through social motivation and self-sacrifice.

Ben was never one to demand credit for the efforts which he initiated. His strategy, rather, was to nettle more conservative individuals into carrying through a campaign which he had launched. Well known to members of the press with whom he daily associated at the National Press Club, he exerted a substantial influence upon national affairs.

Ben was at his best in Congressional hearings. As time passed, some committee chairmen who had faced his incisive criticisms were prone to place his appearance at the end of a crowded agenda. Once on the stand, after long hours of waiting, he drew heavily upon his missionary background by employing telling scriptural references which, while recognizable, might deviate somewhat from the King James version. He coined apt phrases, and called attention to basic issues which otherwise would have remained unmentioned. Well acquainted with committee members, he understood their limitations and the pressure groups to which they were responsive. Not infrequently a hearing would develop so that Ben would be asking the questions and the committee members would be undertaking to defend their actions. To observers who had listened to hours of droning, uninspired statements, Ben's appearance was like a refreshing, late-afternoon cocktail. He was always sincere, his attitude polite and disarming, and the interest which he represented was unique.

Ben was as careful to employ democratic procedures in running the People's Lobby as he was to husband its meager finances. Annual meetings of the Lobby were not well attended. Yet with the greatest care Ben would prepare the agenda, fill it with a record of the year's work, and seek a consensus for the next year's program. Letters from members received careful attention from the Board. Each year, an enlarged program was optimistically projected.

One of Ben's most telling techniques was to make direct inquiries of high government officers and then to issue a press release containing the questions asked and the replies received. He would, for example, ask the Secretary of the Treasury for an explanation of fiscal policy; he would ask the President just what was to be done with the assets of German cartels; he would ask the Bureau of Standards whether they would release the results of their tests so that consumers might benefit from them; he would ask the Secretary of Agriculture to explain the rationale of restricting crop production at a time when people were hungry. The very inadequacy of the ordinary replies was revealing, and especially so when accompanied by Ben's caustic comments.

Many of Ben's most effective releases were associated with heated issues of the hour. It is difficult in retrospect to recapture the atmosphere in which these sallies were issued. Much of the force of the original statements has been lost with the passage of time. In Washington life he was a "character." Reporters came to expect a telling headline, a challenging opening sentence, an unexpected turn of phrase, a pungent quotation, a lively controversial item. He knew news values. Indeed, when evacuated from one office, he even issued a well-publicized release asking President Truman for space in the White House as an appropriate place in which to lodge the People's Lobby.

During three decades in which American public life seemed singularly devoid of statesmen, he found many effective targets. The New Deal, he felt, fell pitifully short as a remedy for American ills. Ben called it a means of "passing the buck to Providence and the bill to posterity." As organized labor and organized farmers found increasing power, he grew ever more restless as he watched them accept government assistance without incorporating his concepts of basic and comprehensive economic reform.

Looking back upon the record of the People's Lobby, Ben's greatest contribution lay perhaps in his stress upon the futility of financing defense, war, and relief programs by continually expanding the national debt. Few months went by without his close scrutiny of Federal fiscal policy, which seemed to him designed to allow high income groups to escape carrying their appropriate share of the tax load. Equally emphasized was the role of land and natural resources in national prosperity. Ben was ever on the lookout for an opportunity to stress the importance of conserving for the people our national heritage. In Ben's mind, the New Deal did not wish to come to grips with the question of wealth distribution, land ownership, and taxation. It was a series of political improvisations. In world terms, Ben felt that there could be no lasting peace unless the resources were socially owned and equitably allocated by an international body. Cartels, monopolies, and tariffs must likewise be tackled on an international basis, if effective results were to be attained.

Ben Marsh worked incessantly to secure the cooperation of other reform groups in backing the broad general goals championed by his organization. Annually, he dispatched copies of his program to major groups and individually solicited the support of community leaders. As America became more conservative, his overtures were most commonly greeted by silence or by polite refusals. Many liberals felt him to be out of step with the times. Agriculture had become "business minded" and restrictive; labor had become preoccupied with business unionism. In the flood of war-induced inflation and prosperity, the reforming zeal of these groups dwindled.

It is very well for those of us who shared in the work of the People's Lobby to applaud the work of Ben Marsh, his diligence, his foresight and his integrity. He left his mark. In all justice, however, we must add a word concerning our own failure. The People's Lobby ceased its corporate existence on October 31, 1950. No acceptable person could be found to carry on its work. And, in the current climate of opinion, it would be difficult to find anyone who could command the allegiance of the People's Lobby membership and Board. By 1950, the flood of reaction had so frightened liberals that only a Ben Marsh could continue to hold the ranks of People's Lobby supporters intact. Another person, even of similar views, would not be possessed of his mellow temperament or of his willingness to live on a pittance. To have no voice at all seemed, in the mood of the time, better than to have a voice which imperfectly reflected the divergent and often intolerant assessments of our international perplexities. We are thus left today with big industry, big agriculture, and big labor as the substantial contesting economic voices in Washington. Ben Marsh is conspicuous by his absence. The future is not happy to contemplate.

COLSTON E. WARNE

Amherst, Massachusetts

Foreword

Lobbying is now one of America's largest industries. It has become a substitute for responsible party government, instead of an adjunct to democratic processes.

The three great bulwarks of reaction in America today are organized religion, organized labor and organized farmers. There are "heretics" in all these classes—men and women with vision, conscience and courage who challenge economic injustices even though they are among the beneficiaries—but the majority don't want the boat rocked, as long as they are comfortable in it.

The church, labor, farm and county press, though chiefly weekly, semi-monthly and monthly, has as large a circulation as metropolitan papers, and could be controlled by the readers.

This book is not an attempt to show up "wicked" members of legislative bodies, including Congress, but to show

1

the responsibility of church, labor and farm organizations for present conditions and dangers. America suffers today as much from mental torpitude as from moral turpitude.

The dictionary defines a "Lobby" as "the persons engaged in lobbying with a particular legislative or deliberative body; also in general, the persons collectively, not members, who strive to influence the action of such a body at any time," and a "Lobbyist" as "one engaged in Lobbying as a business."

The lobbying I did during fifty years varied from working for medical, educational and industrial foreign missions, and asking a handout from the State Legislature for the Pennsylvania Society for the Prevention of Cruelty to Children, in Philadelphia, to working in Albany for tax measures, tenement house reform and municipal ownership, and in Washington—until the People's Lobby became deactivized in October 1950—for and against tax measures, for a Government Marketing Corporation, public ownership of natural resources, monopolies and basic industries, against peacetime universal compulsory military training, and for international organization and controls.

These fifty years have seen vast changes in America, as in the world. America has slowly evolved from our national slogan of "individual aggrandizement and collective irresponsibility" to recognition of Government's larger functions —but wholly inadequate measures to meet them. President Taft, who like Wilson was radical because logical, foresaw the changes when, noting in his speech at Winona, Minnesota, in 1909, that the good free land of the nation had gone into private hands, he warned that this would mean drastic changes in national policies. Both the Roosevelts, however, were highly emotional, and primarily politicians.

During my forty-three years of active lobbying, starting with the New York Committee on Congestion of Population in March 1907, I worked with small groups of people who were not afraid to question and to pioneer and were willing to pay the price of the slow methods of education, implicit in democratic processes to which they were fully committed, but who realized the perils of procrastination. The budgets of organizations for which I worked on salary during these forty-three years did not much exceed an average of about $8,500 a year, though I was sometimes accused of getting a salary of $25,000!

Pioneers don't belong in the get-rich class.

On these small budgets we sent out over one and a half million pieces of literature, including reprints of our material read into the *Congressional Record* (for which we paid), conducted all our campaigns, and between 1931 and 1950 issued a monthly eight-page printed *Bulletin*. All but one of our few large contributions—of four figures—were made by the daughters of rich Republicans. The daughters brought forth fruits meet for their fathers' repentance—to help change our economic system.

Methods of lobbying are diverse. Basically, all education on economic questions is a form of lobbying, at least indirectly, since people's minds are influenced and their will to action aroused by what they hear, see or read. An evidence is the 1945 success of the British Labor Party, which had conducted an intensive educational campaign for nearly forty years.

Technically, the Federal Government makes a sharp distinction. Contributions to organizations which appear before legislative committees and government departments regularly, and otherwise seek to influence them, are not deductible for income taxes. This was the status of the People's

Lobby, and cost it several large contributions; for it refused to organize a tax evading agency, despite the fact the major part of its work was educational in the technical sense.

The Federal Reorganization Act of 1946 requires the registration of all persons devoting a major part of their activities to influencing legislation, and a quarterly report of expenditures itemized as to amounts over $10, with names of all contributors of $500 and over, cumulative for the year. People's Lobby never found this requirement as to contributors any chore since usually about five sixths of our income was from memberships of $5 or less.

This Act, supposed to extract information revealing the actual expenditures of those registered to influence legislation, ignores the hundreds of millions of dollars spent annually on advertising the good old "American Way," and on publications, and the work, whether volunteer or paid, done by members of organized industry, organized labor and organized farmers to induce Members of Congress to see things the way the pleaders do, and the cocktail parties and dinners and other sentiment-swaying devices to mellow opposition and expand support. Lobbyists reported expenditures of $6,-392,622 to influence legislation during the 1st Session of the 81st Congress (nine months) in 1949. This was only a fraction of the total, but the law was, substantially, complied with.

It is not lobbyists who threaten the welfare of the nation, but the fact neither major party has control of its members and neither has a concrete economic program adequate to cope with the problems of a mechanized era, with atomic energy released, but is instead relying for votes upon the ineptness of its opponent, in lulling the public into acquiescence in futile makeshifts.

Fortunately for the American people, the House Select

Committee to Investigate Lobbying Activities, of which Hon. Frank Buchanan of Pennsylvania was Chairman, had a different view of "UnAmerican Activities" than the House Committee with that designation. As member of a panel in a television program in Washington early in 1950, at which Representative Buchanan explained the task of his Committee, I made the appraisal of the Lobbying Act above, and said, frankly, that the Committee would be derelict in its duty unless it investigated these aspects of lobbying. It did so as to expenditures for publications, but not as to advertising.

Most of my work has been pioneering. One syndicated columnist over thirty years ago stated I kept "about two thousand years ahead of the progressives in Congress." That indicates how much behind the times Congress keeps.

The charge is in large measure due to the fact that the three men who have most influenced my thinking were philosophers, not lobbyists: Professor Jesse Macy at Grinnell College (Iowa) who taught me political economy; Dr. Simon Nelson Patten, with whom I took courses in economics for three years in the Graduate School of the University of Pennsylvania, and John Dewey.

Jesse Macy was a farm bred Quaker whose family were pioneer settlers in Iowa, long, lank, slow spoken and slow to wrath, but capable of his full share of righteous indignation when it was called for.

Simon Patten had a similar background in Illinois, like Jesse Macy's, broadened by years of study and travel in Europe. His intellectual hobby—advocacy of the pleasure economy of abundance instead of the pain economy of scarcity—challenged the doleful brutality of the standardized economists of his day, and anticipated the "New Deal" by three decades. He disliked dramatics as much as conformity, and was as similar in manner as in physique to Jesse Macy, both at the head of their profession. He warned me at the close of my academic work with him that it wouldn't be any use for me to take the examinations for my doctorate for he knew the answers I'd make, and I wouldn't be granted the degree signifying mental acquiescence in an out-worn economic system. I passed up the examinations and have managed to survive without a doctorate!

John Dewey, who followed my pioneer work in the Society to Protect Children from Cruelty in Philadelphia, was incisive and radical, because logical. He knew systems, like men, must prove merit, and in his five years as President of People's Lobby he applied the pragmatic test to current issues and policies.

They all lived Dr. Patten's dictum, "Faith is unimpeded tendency to activity." I have tried to.

Shortly before the elder Senator Robert M. LaFollette's death, I went to see him about some measure in his Committee room, following a strenuous Senate session. He was lying on his couch, puffing at his pipe, then turned to me and remarked: "Ben, I believe in democracy, but will it ever *work?*"

I was almost paralyzed by the query.

Here was a man who had devotedly worked for the people throughout his entire life at personal sacrifice, for he would have made much more either as a practicing lawyer or an actor—who had fought for civil liberties, literally taking his life in his hands during World War One—and had never faltered in his courage. He was close to seventy, but still vigorous, though much depressed over the results of his 1924 campaign for the Presidency.

I would now answer Senator LaFollette's question about as

follows: "No kind of democracy can work, unless the intelligence, integrity and information of the people are equal to the responsibilities which democracy imposes on the people."

Senator LaFollette was not alone. In 1937, Lawrence Dennis' book "The Coming American Fascism" took the position America couldn't make the necessary economic changes without an authoritarian government. This was so challenging I thought it merited a radio debate and asked Sen. Hugo Black (now Mr. Justice Black) whether he would take the negative. He promptly agreed to, but I suggested he read Dennis' book first, as Dennis would ask him some embarrassing questions on the radio. He read the book and declined to debate, stating, "That fellow knows what he is talking about." Justice Black, as well as Senator Black, has well sustained the best traditions of both economic and political democracy.

My philosophy of life was attained at the ripe maturity of seventeen years, when in 1894 my "graduation" oration as Senior Prep, at Grinnell College Academy in Iowa, was titled "Ye Fates Farewell." It did not win First Prize, with its claim that the individual and society had to work out their own destiny without too much reliance upon any unseen power. It shocked some of the sincere conformists who cherished a consoling conviction of life, and of hell-fire everlasting for those who questioned any of the "eternal verities."

The rate of human progress seems largely determined by such challenge—in the quest for certainty.

Because I have always spoken for groups to whom God gave it to see the right, as he gave to too few others, my position has been anomalous, particularly in Washington. I frequently stated to Congressional Committees that we hadn't a large enough membership to threaten them with, and had no money, so I had to ask them to consider a measure on its merits. This was a more revolutionary doctrine than the "dictatorship of the proletariat," not because it was beyond the mental capacity of most members of Congress but because it was loaded politically.

I have testified at several hundred Congressional Committee hearings in my nearly thirty-three years residence in Washington, starting in March, 1918. In general, I found the conservative members afraid *not* to be polite to me because I had a flair for publicity, and the liberals afraid *to* be polite to me lest they be tarred also with premature intelligence, which is supposed to be an insult to your constituents.

The conservatives were usually much surer of themselves, they had better organizations and they could bring more "bacon" to the home districts than the liberals, and that is the great test of statesmanship. Usually, conservatives kept their agreements better, also, because they have no reason to be scared of what national or local propaganda for the "American Way" could do to their constituents.

Few members of the People's Lobby were extremists and few believed in either the Euclidean inexorabilities of the Marxian dogma, or the divine origin of the system of private profits. Most were economic pragmatists, and the Lobby worked continuously for a mixed economy—public, cooperative and private ownership, but inclusively, under an overall Government plan.

Members of Congress would almost always listen to my statements at Committee hearings, and used to ask me many questions, but since World War Two started they have been chary about this, probably fearing my answers would tend to degrade and incriminate the Congress of the United States. They often would have.

In 1950, when I wrote Chairman Robert L. Doughton of

the House Ways and Means Committee that I would like to appear on a Revenue measure, he replied that he personally would like to have me, because "your statements are always intelligent and sincere." A little earlier Senator Joseph C. O'Mahoney asked in a public hearing, what was the use of all my appearances since Congress didn't accept our program. I replied that was the fault of Congress, and his statement indicted both major parties. He didn't challenge that charge.

Reform comes hard in a nation where most of the "have nots" are extremely anxious to get into the class they are most vigorously damning, and expect Congress to enact legislation to enable them to do so.

In America, malefactors of great wealth are no longer a real threat. The real threat is the many millions of would-be wealthy, not through their production and effort, but through government help.

Just for the record, among the things that organizations for which I have been spokesman have worked for, with others, are:

City planning.
Progressive personal income and profits taxes.
Public ownership of power and other natural resources.
Federal old age pensions.
Federal unemployment insurance.
Public works.
Farm resettlement projects.
Public housing.
Federal relief.
Pure food and drug laws.
Civil rights
Price fixing and rationing.

Protective labor legislation, including a shorter work
week.

International cooperation and organization.

This book is largely a story about that work.

Thurman Arnold, in his book "The Folklore of Capitalism" quotes, as proof I am a realist, my statement to a Senate
Committee in the early thirties that we favored the thirty
hour week though it wouldn't do much good, "but in America we won't do anything intelligent as long as there is
something foolish we can do."

Whatever Russia has done, or not done, she has shortened
the time America can postpone doing certain inevitable intelligent things.

I was the first lobbyist to register under the new lobbying
act (Reorganization Act) of 1946, which resulted in my being
dubbed "America's Number One Lobbyist" in nation-wide
publicity, and that made me the most publicized, though I
continued to be the poorest-paid, lobbyist in the Nation's
Capital.

Any conclusions I draw are of course my own, and no former officer or member of any organization for which I have
lobbied can be criticized therefor.

In the fall of 1891, fresh from the Peasant State, Bulgaria,
and wearing my first "boughten" suit, made of the native
cloth, when I went into the office of the Principal of Grinnell College Academy to register, I saw on his desk two lines
from Matthew Arnold I have never forgotten:

> *But tasks in hours of insight willed,*
> *May be through years of gloom fulfilled.*

B. C. M.

Washington, D.C.

CHAPTER ONE

Education of a Lobbyist

No LIFE ACTIVITY can be fully understood without at least a reference to what the life sprang from.

My parents, Ursula Clarke Marsh and Rev. George D. Marsh, of New England stock, were missionaries under the Congregationalist American Board of Commissioners for Foreign Missions. My mother, one of the early graduates of Mt. Holyoke College, went to Brousa in Asia Minor in 1868 as a teacher in the Congregationalist Mission. My father, a graduate of Grinnell College, about the same time went to Turkey for evangelistic work, and they met in Constantinople, but went to the present Bulgaria after marriage.

Of the four children, of whom I was the second, I was the black sheep—and disliked the color line then, also. My parents' acquired theology was pretty dour; their innate compassion and humanism was unfailing, and this, not their theology, won friends and converts.

My earliest childhood recollection is the agonized and effective screams of my mother, when some Turkish irregular troops tried to kidnap me—a five year old—from the little Turkish village in the Rhodope Mountains near Philip-popolis where we spent one summer. Our Turkish neighbors effected my release, promptly. The second thrill was running away, three years later in 1885, to try to be a drummer boy in the Bulgarian Army, when Servia attacked my pro-tem land. Bulgarian officers promptly returned me to my parents who used orthodox methods to convince me that foreign missionary progeny should be neutral abroad.

The summer I graduated from Grinnell College in 1898, I became assistant State Secretary of the Y.M.C.A. in Iowa, in charge of the college work, and I also had the job of rais-ing a good part of the budget through visiting some hun-dred places, big and little, throughout the State. In those days State Y.M.C.A. workers, as well as ministers, had passes on most railroads.

My first criticism came from the International College Y.M.C.A. Secretary, when he received reports from certain of the Institutions of Higher Learning in that Prairie State that I was talking social economics. His advice to me was, "You let the professors of political economy tend to teaching the boys economics, and you devote yourself to saving their souls." I did not accept this injunction. Our college Presi-dent George A. Gates, earlier a Congregationalist Minister, once said in college chapel, "A man who worries about sav-ing his own soul hasn't a soul that's worth saving."

My State Board was very kind, wanted me to stay a second year, offering a big increase in salary as they told me I was "a good money raiser." I declined the invitation and took a year's work in the Graduate School at Chicago University in economics, sociology and history, earning my way there as I had in the seven years at Grinnell.

The two following years were given to raising money for foreign missions of the American Board. In this I was associated with the late Luther D. Wishard, who started the "Forward Movement" in that Board, as he had started the College Y.M.C.A. in 1877. The second year, on nearly every Sunday of the heavy church-going part of the year, I succeeded in raising the salary for a foreign missionary in some church, though I confined myself to men or women engaged in educational, industrial or medical work—one of America's great services to the world. That was a sincere "Point Four," with no thought of profits to be made by business follow-ups.

During those two years I visited most of the large industrial cities of New England and New York, and made occasional visits to Philadelphia, Washington and Middle Western cities, as far as Eau Claire, Wisconsin. Even in those early 1900's there were many ministers with the social conscience of Graham Taylor of Chicago and of Washington Gladden of Columbus, Ohio, both of whom had stirred us students in Grinnell. Many sincere Christian ministers I met recognized fully then the terrible industrial conditions in Fall River, New Bedford, Lawrence, Lowell and other textile centers, and most of them admitted they were afraid to speak out about them.

In college I had become a member of the Student Volunteers and was all set, after finishing my graduate work, to go as a teacher somewhere in the Dark Continent. After seeing conditions in our industrial centers, I decided I need not cross the ocean to work in a Dark Continent.

In 1902 I accepted a fellowship (tuition and $600.00 a year) in the Graduate School of the University of Pennsylvania, to study the homeless man and how he was treated. Much of my work was done under Professor Patten, then about fifty and well established and esteemed despite his eco-

nomic unorthodoxy. My field work was under the direction
of Mary E. Richmond, Secretary of the Pennsylvania Society
for Organizing Charity. Her frequently emphasized principle was to do for each family in distress what seemed the
best thing under the circumstances. I could not think of anything more stupid, for it seemed only common sense to
question why so many families were so frequently in distress,
and to determine how to stop it.

I raised money for the Charity Organization Society, interviewed derelicts at its Wayfarers' Lodge, and tried to get
the anti-begging ordinances enforced. The Philadelphia papers soon nick-named me "The Terror of the Tramp." In
the summer of 1903 I went to Europe to study methods of
caring for ordinary tramps, and the ways of what were
known as "Consular Tramps," who sponged on our Consuls
to see Europe.

That fall I was elected Secretary of the Pennsylvania Society to Protect Children from Cruelty. There I had my first
direct lobbying, though you could call it lobbying to get the
money out of the pockets of the poor for humanitarian foreign missions, and out of the pockets of the wealthy for sweet
and stultifying charity. Part of my lobbying was trying to get
at least $2,500 to $3,000 every two years out of the Pennsylvania Legislature for the "Cruelty to Children." We had
some good Republican politicians on the Board, which
helped quite a bit, and we always got the money.

Those were the early days of social work. When I went
into the "Cruelty to Children," it had two broken down ex-
policemen as agents, who were quite as human when they
were half-seas over as when sober. In the three and a half
years I was there, we changed that; and when I left there was
a force of about 30 including several well-trained college
men and women, among others Ada Hopkins, sister of Harry

Hopkins, later to be famous as relief head in the New Deal as well as Secretary of Commerce and the President's courier to Europe.

The organization had limited but effective police powers, under which we were able to get the required consent of parents to let their children have needed medical care and operations, and most of the 900 to 1,000 children involved in cases brought to us every year needed one or both.

We also ended, while I was Secretary, the practice of sending children committed to the Society to crowded institutions, where the death rate was terrifying and personalities almost wholly suppressed. By the end of my second year every child in our charge, except where custodial care was imperative, was placed in a private home in the country. We helped the parent or parents placed in our probation to get a job, and had them pay as much as possible for their children's board until they were sufficiently rehabilitated to have their children back, under supervision.

Our program saved the city and private charities at least $150,000 a year—and proved that ten days to six months in jail for parents, and a longer commitment to institutions for children, is *not* the way to prevent cruelty to children.

I also pioneered medical examination of children in the public schools and school lunches for them, with the active help of Dr. Talcott Williams, then editor of the Philadelphia *Press* and later head of the School of Journalism at Columbia University.

My Board was shocked by my advocacy of old age pensions and unemployment insurance at a National Conference of Charities and Correction.

During these years I was carrying nearly full graduate work at the University of Pennsylvania. I also did some lobbying for child-welfare legislation, to help Scott Nearing, who was for part of the time Secretary of the Pennsylvania Child Labor Committee.

My work for better housing got me in very dutch with some of my Board, who either owned slum properties themselves or who had friends deeply interested in them, and I was given a choice of shut up or get out. Our parting was mutually agreeable; as I could not accept the view that because relieving suffering gave more pleasure to the well-to-do than preventing it, they were entitled to insist upon continuing misery to be relieved, rather than preventing it. The Board, however, offered to increase my salary by one half if I would be conformist—but the lure was not alluring.

Bread upon the Waters

IN THE EARLY WINTER of 1907, Mary K. Simkhovitch, Director of Greenwich House, Florence Kelley, Secretary of the National Consumers League, Lillian D. Wald, head of the Nurses Settlement and Home Nursing Service, Reverend Gaylord S. White of Union Theological Seminary and Union Settlement, and Dr. Hermon C. Bumpus, Director of the American Museum of Natural History, among the alert social-minded citizens of New York, organized a Committee on Congestion of Population in New York. Their plan was to put on an exhibit showing the terrible conditions, hoping to lead the city authorities to more basic action than any tenement-house legislation or social action attempted up to then.

In February that year the Committee asked me to be secretary and I accepted, starting work March first. That summer I went to Europe to gather material in Germany, Britain, France and elsewhere, on city planning and housing, attending an international housing conference in London that

17

summer. When I returned the "1907 Panic" was under way. The Committee, of which Dr. Bumpus was Chairman, got scared and decided that we would have to give up the exhibit. It looked that way.

At this point Miss Carola Woerishoffer, whom I had recently met at Bryn Mawr where she was a senior and who was keenly interested in our work, asked me what was the minimum amount on which I would go ahead and organize the exhibit. I told her $3,000, and she pledged that amount. She paid it on the dot.

The exhibit held in the American Museum of Natural History in March 1908 was a distinct success from every point of view—except producing action to remedy the conditions shown! Governor Charles E. Hughes made the key speech at the opening session of the Conference. For about three-quarters of an hour before the meeting I took him through the exhibit, which filled most of one of the big wings of the Museum, pointing out the most striking features.

He was much struck with a huge paste-board cube representing the then assessed value of land in Manhattan, about $2,800,000,000, and on the top a diminutive ivory cube representing the $28.00 paid the Indians for Manhattan Island in 1626.

In his speech deploring the conditions in New York's congested areas, Governor Hughes stressed the fact that we had not begun to realize what the State could do to remedy and end social injustices through the taxing power of the State. Unfortunately some wealthy people did realize just what the State could do in this way and, being the State, they saw to it that the State did not in any way interfere with their legalized rackets.

Following the Congestion exhibit, the Committee on Con-

gestion of Population in New York got Governor Hughes to create a Commission on Distribution of Population, to study methods of securing a more efficient placement of people. Mr. V. Everit Macy was Chairman, and among the members were Judge Adelbert Moot of Buffalo, Dr. Stephen S. Wise, and members of the Congestion Committee, while I was Secretary.

The Committee held hearings, studied various projects, and in its report advocated more control over location of factories (startling suggestion), State aid to resettlement, and shifting taxation from labor products to land values, as well as the old-line methods of trying to beat the devil around a bush. I was made Secretary of the Commission, without salary, and saw Governor Hughes in his private office in Albany several times in connection with the Commission's work.

I was in his office there the morning the papers announced that he was being considered for appointment (the first time) to the Supreme Court. He remarked to me that if people knew how radical he really was they would not want him on the Supreme Court. I wished him the best of success on the bench.

The Honorable Lawson Purdy, then President of the City Board of Taxes and Assessments, had given me great help in studying the land-values and land problem of Greater New York, pointing out the effect of taxing buildings at the same rate as land values in creating speculative land values, encouraging slums, and discouraging the construction of healthy buildings.

Following the exhibit in the Natural History Museum, parts of it were taken to Brooklyn and shown as a warning of what might happen to that Borough.

Within a short time, advocates of higher taxation of land

values and exemption of buildings from taxation organized
the Society to Lower Rents and Reduce Taxes on Homes in
New York. Frederic C. Leubuscher, a prominent attorney,
was President of this Organization, of which I was unpaid
Secretary, and it made a militant campaign for the transfer
of taxes on buildings to land values, cooperating with the
Congestion Committee, which worked also for city planning
and zoning of the city.

Following the Congestion exhibit, Raymond V. Ingersoll,
outstanding in civic affairs in the city and later Park Commissioner and President of the Borough of Brooklyn, was
Chairman of the Committee. He was a genius in stating facts
and getting cooperation. At that time we had a deficit of
$1,500, which his wife generously paid to give us a fresh
start.

The measure that aroused the most discussion in those
years was a carefully drafted bill providing for a city referendum on gradually transferring taxes on buildings in New
York City to land values. Strange as it may seem, this bill
was introduced in the Senate by "Big Tim" Sullivan, one
of the stalwarts of Tammany Hall, and in the Assembly by
Assemblyman Brooks, a Republican from a silk-stocking district in the middle west-side of Manhattan.

"Big Tim" lived on the Bowery, where I had to go to see
him occasionally. He was a physical giant, hot tempered but
not nursing grudges. He was constantly attacked by the politicians, who charged him with most of the misdemeanors
and worse, of which politicians do not have a monopoly. I
knew him well, seeing him frequently in his apartment on
the Bowery, where his "bodyguard" let me through to discuss tactics in connection with our campaign to tax land
values more.

Once when the papers made a particularly vicious attack

upon him, I asked him why he didn't sue them for libel. His answer was characteristic: "Begorra I ought to, but they might up and prove it on me."

In the campaign for our bill, I spoke one to ten times in every Assembly District of the five Boroughs of Greater New York. It was of course fought tooth and nail by the real-estate interests which specialized in land speculation, and almost equally hard by the loaning interests, which claimed that it would suddenly wipe out all selling price of land in New York City and make every life insurance policy and savings account worthless. Fortunately few of those claiming this really believed it.

Outstanding opponents of the measure included Mr. Allan Robinson, President of the New York Real Estate Board, who sometimes met us in debate but more often had a free field in picturing the horrors which would result from the proposed plan. Mr. Walter Stabler, Comptroller of the Metropolitan Life Insurance Co., was leader and organizer of the opposition by the lending interests.

The *coup-de-grâce* was given to the measure by Alfred E. Smith, who was majority leader in the Assembly. Following repeated hearings before the Committees of both branches of the Legislature, it seemed certain that we had sufficient votes to get the bill reported out and force a record vote, as Al Smith had agreed to do this. To my dismay, one afternoon the Chairman of the Committee told me that Al had reversed himself and decided not to let the bill out of Committee.

Naturally I saw Al at once, taxed him with double crossing me, which he admitted. I asked him why he had done it. He was perfectly frank, and stated that certain interests were opposed to it. I was equally frank and told him that I knew the Catholic Church and some wealthy families owned much valuable land in the City, but I was dealing with him as an official and not a Catholic. He admitted this was just. I reminded him that the bill merely provided for a referendum of the voters in New York City, and he said, "Yes, I know that, but I am going to save my people the trouble of thinking about it. I will do the thinking for them. Besides I am afraid they would vote for it if they got the chance." Our lobbying had produced results.

An important step in trying to get the conscience of New York hurting enough to get it to do something about housing and congestion was taken when Mayor William J. Gaynor, Tammany candidate elected in 1909, appointed a City Commission on Congestion of Population. This was backed not only by the civic organizations but by many real-estate and loaning interests, who hoped apparently that with sufficient conservative members the Commission would report something less scaring than rigid control of height and cubage of buildings, reducing the per cent of the lot that could be occupied by buildings, and gradual transfer of taxes on buildings to land values, which the New York Congestion Committee and the Lower Rents Society so vigorously advocated.

The Mayor appointed the Commission with his blessing, but the Board of Aldermen failed to make any appropriation therefor. The Honorable Jacob Cantor, former President of the Borough of Manhattan and a loyal but shrewd member of Tammany Hall, was made Chairman, while the best known member of the Commission was Dr. Frank J. Goodnow, Professor of Constitutional Law at Columbia University (later President of Johns Hopkins), who was at the time Chairman of the Congestion Committee. The Commission included Republican and Democratic members of the Board of Aldermen, held frequent meetings, and took its job very seriously. Professor Goodnow with all his erudition and experience was as good a mixer as any man could be, and won not only the respect but the admiration of the most conservative Tammany members of the Commission. He was Chairman of the Committee on Taxation.

In a modest way, the Commission was a precursor of several national Commissions of Inquiry. Its chief recommendations were for more control of construction to ensure better living conditions, extension of public ownership of transportation, and provision of freight belt lines, etc., higher income taxes, reducing the tax rate on buildings to half that on land values, a land increment tax, and ("believe it or not") widows' pensions.

Some of the private charities in the city strenuously opposed widows' pensions, even as recently as 1910, but their objections did not impress the Tammany Hall or Republican members of the Commission, who as Aldermen could see the votes as well as the merits in the plan. Their comments on the representatives of private charities who opposed such public pensions and other social measures would have made very interesting reading, but they were very carefully excised by the Commission.

The report was formal, running to 270-odd pages, including appendices with tables.

As Secretary of the Commission, I had a double job: to help run the show; and also unfortunately, as the un-official Congestion Committee was broke, to finance the costs of the city Commission out of my private deficit. It was probably just as well that I did not attempt to get a salary from it!

When the report was printed, Frank Dowling, Tammany President of the Board of Aldermen, moved that all the reports be thrown in the East River, as a mark of appreciation.

Fortunately the members—both Tammany and Republican—
of the Board of Aldermen, who served on the Commission,
called him effectively, but they were unable to get any appropriation through the Board for the actual expenses of
the Commission. Understanding the absence of vital difference between the Republican and the Tammany Machines
in New York, I got a Republican friend, a very smart lawyer
and East Side boy, to take me to see Charles F. Murphy,
Tammany leader in the Old Wigwam on 14th Street. Only
about five minutes were necessary to convince Mr. Murphy
that it was bad politics at least to refuse to pay the minimum
expenses, which did not include a secretarial salary, for a
Commission appointed by Tammany's Mayor, which recommended widows' pensions. At the next meeting of the Board
of Aldermen the bill of about $1,500 was allowed, my ad-
vances were repaid, and I was able to pay off enough of my
creditors to keep hope alive in the breasts of the rest!

Dr. Goodnow had been a classmate of Charles Pratt,
Treasurer of Standard Oil, and wrote him asking he make
a contribution to the Congestion Committee. Mr. Pratt, in
declining, wrote "I don't believe you know how radical that
man Marsh is, or you wouldn't have anything to do with
him." Dr. Goodnow said, "I'm backing you, but I suppose
we can't expect people to contribute to the cutting of their
financial throats."

One of my most entertaining experiences during eleven
years in New York was being expelled from the Men's City
Club in the spring of 1916, because of my indelicate but
effective method of opposing a franchise sought by the Interborough Rapid Transit Company, which I had adequate
reason to regard as a racket.

I had for several years been a member of the City Club,
and realized that while many members were highly progres-

sive the control did not approve measures which threatened the financial status quo. Hon. Homer Folks, at that time President of the New York State Charities Aid Association, was Chairman of the Transit Committee of the City Club; and Mr. Henry C. Wright, a prominent civic worker and expert on transit matters, was Secretary. Mr. Wright informed me he feared the Committee, and probably the Club, was prepared to approve this franchise, and asked if I would attempt to block it, as both Mr. Folks and he thought it was loaded against the City, a verdict in which I fully concurred.

The newspapers had always been very friendly, not to me personally particularly, but to my somewhat vivid language. In some open letters to the officers of the Club, copies of which I gave to the press, I asked that the officers oppose the franchise, and urged municipal ownership. Since this did not receive a favorable response, the next step was to point out that August Belmont, the financier who had made a fortune out of rapid transit in New York, and Theodore P. Shonts, then President of the Interborough Rapid Transit Company, were influential in the City Club and were apparently using that influence to get endorsement by the Club for the franchise, in which both were interested. The officers of the Club denied the charge and asserted that I had more influence in the Club than either of the two named gentlemen—but they did not oppose the franchise!

My next step was to accuse the Club of being a "home for fallen men," a characterization which rated first-class headlines in most of the city's papers, but did not rate as a measure of pacification. The directors of the Club then informed me that I would be put on trial for conduct unbecoming a member and invited me to appear before them. I replied that the Board favoring such a franchise was guilty of conduct unbecoming members of the Club, and refused

to appear for the trial unless the newspapers were all invited
to send representatives. This also struck fire in the headlines,
as I objected to a "Star Chamber" proceeding.

The Board met and, I think with only one dissenting vote,
formally expelled me from the Club. The franchise, which
was all scheduled to go through, was killed dead as a door-
nail; and I made lots of friends—including many labor leaders—who could not come out in the open. The Board and I
remained on speaking terms and I used the dues saved by my
expulsion for practical purposes.

An incident, not directly connected with lobbying, was my
unexpected witnessing of the attempted assassination of
Mayor William J. Gaynor, as he was about to sail for a
summer vacation in Europe. I had gone to the ship to bid
goodbye to Carola Woerishoffer, bound on a similar trip.
We were standing less than ten feet from the Mayor, who
was talking with the Commissioner of Street Cleaning, Mr.
Edwards, and a Catholic priest, when a disgruntled employee of the Department, mentally deranged, shot the
Mayor, the bullet entering his neck.

Commissioner Edwards, who was next to the assailant, immediately grappled with him and disarmed him, while I
went to the Mayor and asked if I could help him to his stateroom. He accepted and as I started to help him down the
stairs the priest asked him whether he should administer the
last rites, to which the Mayor, a former Catholic, promptly
replied, "No, I am through with that sort of thing."

A photographer got a picture of the Mayor while I was
helping him down, which found a place among famous snap-
shots. As soon as Robert Adamson, the Mayor's Secretary,
brought a doctor to the stateroom, I retired.

Miss Woerishoffer was not at all upset by the proceedings.
She had come away without any American change, and asked

me if I would lend her a dollar until she got back. I complied, though all the money I had in the world at that time was less than $20, and I was several hundred dollars in debt. The first mail after she reached Europe contained a check for $1,000 for the Congestion Committee. That was genuinely casting bread upon the waters. Florence Kelly, founder of Consumers' League, had recently described me as having spent my life quarreling with my bread and butter. I permitted myself an occasional truce.

Among our constructive achievements was development of a national program for city planning. On my trips to Europe in 1907 and 1908, I had collected the material for a small book on European city planning, based upon the experience of Britain, Germany, France, Switzerland, and Belgium. My book, "An Introduction to City Planning," of some 130 pages, was printed privately in 1909. Practically the whole edition of 1,000 was sold within about a year, and has never been reprinted. George B. Ford, later to be famous as Housing Expert and City Planner, had written the chapter on technical architectural features of city planning, which he was eminently qualified to do from his successful experience as an architect.

Following the publication of this book, we arranged a conference on city planning in Washington; and Henry Morgenthau, then Chairman of the Congestion Committee, and I went to Washington to invite President Taft to preside at the meeting. He courteously expressed his great interest in the subject, but explained that Congress was very jealous of having the Chief Executive give it any advice or take the initiative in such a matter. That was only forty years ago! He suggested that the Honorable Richard A. Ballinger, Secretary of the Interior, later to be spot-lighted through his controversy with Gifford Pinchot, Fred Kerby and J. R.

Glavis over disposal of the nation's forest lands, be Chairman of the sessions.

We had already popularized the subject by a city-planning exhibit, which the Congestion Committee sponsored in New York, and by talks on the subject in a series of conferences in New York and other cities. Our Washington conference was eminently successful, and secured nation-wide publicity. Speaker Joe Cannon, often called the "Czar" of the House, spoke at our banquet in the Raleigh Hotel and wished us luck, though not too optimistically.

As a result of this conference, the National City Planning Association was organized and several hundred city and county planning commissions have since been set up. The New York City Planning Commission, set up following our Exhibits, worked out a plan for zoning the city of New York and for restricting commercial buildings, particularly in the business sections, to a certain cubage or volume in relation to the area of the site, with set-backs at a certain height from the street, or alley, or court, to protect light and ventilation. George B. Ford worked out the details of this cubage system.

In my book on city planning, I had stressed the control which British, French, German, Swiss and Belgian municipal authorities had over the development of cities (in Germany particularly, where city planning was most fully developed), and the land increment tax and other measures adopted to reduce the cost of public improvements and to make the main beneficiaries (the land owners) pay the major part of the cost. None of these measures was included in the city planning adopted by American cities. Instead they played up the artistic display features, and the slums continued. Land speculators and bankers had captured the city planning movement.

Mr. Joseph Fels, single-taxer, free-trader and business

man, who was not afraid of his fellow business men, was much interested in the work of the Congestion Committee. Though less than five foot six in height, he used to address his fellow high tariff manufacturers, as "Fellow Thieves."

Henry Morgenthau had a good deal of land in outlying areas in New York. As Chairman, he made a pledge of $1,500 to the Congestion Committee and gave us space for an office in the City Investing Building, which was only partially filled. Shortly after making his pledge, and before redeeming any of it, Mr. Morgenthau became alarmed at the growing sentiment for transferring taxes from buildings to land values in New York. He told me that unless the Committee would stop urging this he would refuse to pay his pledge, and we would have to get out of the City Investing Building, because we were hurting his interests. He had made a lot speculating in urban land.

Naturally I assured him that we would not change our program, but he could resign as Chairman. He did, the pledge remained unpaid, and we moved to less roomy quarters with our convictions and conscience intact, but a more than deflated treasury. I told this story to Joseph Fels, and he promptly offered to give the Congestion Committee $1,000 to sue Henry Morgenthau, Sr., on his welched pledge. It would have been fun, but we did not do it!

After the famous Bull Moose campaign in 1912, we put on a lower-rents exhibit, in our favorite vacant store on Union Square, making a special appeal to tenants in the exhibit, sections of which, like the Congestion exhibit and the City Planning exhibit, were taken to Brooklyn. About every minute during the exhibit a bell rang to indicate that a baby had been born in New York, and that the selling price of land had gone up about $800—that being the average, according to assessed valuation of land in the city.

I wanted very much to have "T.R." (Theodore Roosevelt) endorse the principle of higher taxation of land values than of buildings, and got my friend Paul Kellogg of *Survey Graphic* to introduce me to the Colonel in the *Outlook* office, "T.R." being at the time one of its contributing editors. To my surprise, Kellogg in introducing me to the Colonel remarked that I had supported Wilson instead of him that year. "T.R.," astonished at my unadulterated stupidity, asked me why, and I told him frankly that I did not think he was honest on his economics. "Let's not discuss that," he snapped back. "What do you want me to do for you?"

I told him we wanted him to speak at our lower rents exhibit on how shifting taxes from buildings to land values would encourage construction of more buildings and would lower rents. "Of course, it would," he said, "and I will talk for you." He did, and made a rattling good speech to a fair sized audience, which got splendid publicity. In fact it was a better speech than most he had made that campaign, when he was angling for votes. As much a commentary on voters as on candidates!

T.R.'s campaign for social justice and the welfare state wasn't the first effort to arouse the American people to a sense of social responsibility. Woodrow Wilson as Governor of New Jersey had sponsored several such measures, as well as an effort to curb trusts and corporate growth. The fight he made as Governor to end New Jersey's reputation as "the mother of trusts" was a big asset to him in his advocacy of the "New Freedom."

In 1910, Senator Wm. S. Newlands, Democrat of Nevada, organized a hearing in Washington of the Senate District Committee on municipal housing, at which I advocated it for the District of Columbia, and also transferring taxes on buildings to land values, or a special tax on pure site value in the District. Nothing came of it then, except publicity for the ideas.

Financing any kind of a movement that looks ahead is at best an arduous job. When you are suggesting uprooting the Ark of the Covenant of democracy—or even curbing it, as did the program of the New York Congestion Committee for a city plan including rigid control of the use of land, and transferring taxes on buildings to land values—you are in a highly hazardous occupation. Both measures challenged the divine right of land speculators, and New York City had been the paradise of land speculators for years before the New York Congestion Committee started. Henry George had run for Mayor of New York two decades earlier on the issue; Sam Gompers, for many years President of the American Federation of Labor, had campaigned for him—and Theodore Roosevelt against him.

Probably because Lillian Wald, who started the Visiting Nurses Association and Nurses Settlement on Henry Street in New York's East Side, was an active member of the Congestion Committee, Jacob H. Schiff, Paul Warburg (one of the architects of the Federal Reserve System) and Felix Warburg, all members of the banking firm of Kuhn Loeb and Co., had contributed to the Congestion Committee.

In the spring of 1909, I was invited to speak on social work to the Twentieth Century Club in Boston, and stated my conviction that many directors of charitable and social welfare organizations should be sent to institutions for the feeble minded, or to reformatories. I based my conclusion upon the fact that so many of such directors were officers or directors of some of the great looting institutions of America. The word "subversive" had not yet wormed its way into general use to characterize a person who dissents from the status quo and challenges its divine origin, but the New York as well as the Boston papers played up my remarks, with double column headlines, and I was a marked person.

Some months later it became my sad duty to try to get Jacob Schiff and the two Warburgs to renew their sizable contributions to the Committee, and with memories of the story of Daniel in the lions' den, I phoned them for appointments. Mr. Schiff and Paul Warburg begged to be excused, and being a beggar myself I had to grant the request, but Felix Warburg's secretary made an appointment for me to see him. My funny-bone warned me I was going to have a bad time.

Mr. Warburg looked at me quizically when I was convoyed into his presence, and started conversation by picking up a bunch of clippings from Boston and New York papers lying on his desk, which he showed me and asked whether I had made the reported statement about directors of charitable and social welfare organizations. I not only admitted I had, but gave him quite a talk on the futility of trying to prevent the spread of tuberculosis while millions of people were packed in dark tenements and undernourished, and the folly of relying upon private charity to meet the tragedies of unemployment—a subject upon which I had a vigorous discussion some two decades later in Washington with Walter S. Gifford, when he was heading up President Hoover's Committee to stimulate private action to meet the unemployment situation through charity, in the peak of the Great Depression.

I also told Felix Warburg that the way Kuhn Loeb and Co. had handled the finances of one of the great transcontinental railroads seemed to me more like buccaneering than proper financing, and gave him details. I left empty handed, but felt that I had done my duty.

One Sunday shortly after the sinking of the *Lusitania,* on a week-end up at a social-workers camp near Hartsdale, a short distance north of New York, a group of us were walking by permission through Felix Warburg's beautiful estate when we met him driving a thoroughbred in a two-wheeled gig. I waved to him, and was astounded when he stopped his horse and said, "Mr. Marsh could I speak to you a minute?"

"Of course," I replied as the rest of our bunch walked on, wondering not only that he remembered me, though I was in the papers a lot, but what he had in mind after our discussion in the offices of Kuhn Loeb and Co. a few years before.

"Marsh," he said, "I have a nephew in the German navy and a close relative in the American navy and I don't want either of them killed—can't you stop this war?"

Lack of words has seldom been one of my failings, but that time I was for a few seconds completely speechless, staring at him.

There was no question of his earnestness and sincerity, his face was haggard and drawn.

"Mr. Warburg," I answered, "why do you ask me, practically a nobody, to stop this war, when the big international bankers, some of whom you must know, are as much responsible as anyone for it?"

He mentioned the campaigns to prevent war and to block our entrance into it with a blank check signed, in which I had helped, as reported in the press.

"Of course," I told him, "I'll do all I can to stop this and any war."

He thanked me sincerely.

I might have told him he should take his medicine, but all

my life whenever I tangled with a multi-millionaire, or just a garden variety of millionaire, I remembered the words of John Wesley when he saw a condemned criminal on his way to execution: "There, but for the grace of God, go I." Had I been born as they had been, I would probably—yes, almost certainly—have done as they did, and it would have been just as stupid. But I could never see how in a nation with a free vote, except in the few poll-tax states, the voters could fairly blame the rich for their actions, when they could set the standards and enforce them with their votes. This would be much easier, admittedly, under a system of responsible Party Government, such as the British.

While it is true that the blood of the kickers is the seed of reform, it is equally true that in America a good many kickers—reformers—are extremely anxious to get into the class they are most vigorously damning. They want to abolish classes by getting into the class they want to abolish. That's one way to do it!

I have told how generously Carola Woerishoffer supported the New York Congestion Committee, not only with her money, but with active and highly intelligent work. Not long after our successful Congestion Exhibit, I told her jokingly that I probably ought to pay her the compliment of asking her to marry me, as I was sure she had too much sense to accept me, but instead I promised to use the money she gave the Congestion Committee to try to end the system which gave her her wealth, and protected it, and the first step was a very progressive Federal income tax and government controls. That was long before the Sixteenth Amendment.

She rubbed her hands together gleefully, her habit when she was particularly pleased, and said: "That's the best use to which my money could be put."

After her death, one of her friends informed me that she had planned to set up a fund which would give me an income of $2,000 a year—which was more than the salary I was getting—but she hadn't made a codicil to her will, and it fell through. Probably this was best for me; because such a windfall, so early in my life, might have made me lazy, and as my College President once said in chapel, "There's hope for the vicious boy, but none for the lazy."

Within reason there's no substitute for the American saying, "Root hog, or die," or as earlier expressed: "If any man will not work, neither shall he eat." The human race is now rather unsuccessfully trying to devise a system by which the "hog" is enabled to root, and man to work, and get enough out of it to give him and his dependents a decent standard of living.

Soon after going to New York I met Lawrence Veiller, a pioneer in tenement house reform, with Jacob A. Riis. He took me later to see Robert W. de Forrest, an extremely able lawyer, first Tenement House Commissioner in New York City, who had been personal counsel to Russell Sage. Mr. de Forrest was first Chairman of the Russell Sage Foundation, set up by Mr. Sage's widow out of his vast wealth. Mr. Veiller told Mr. de Forrest I was stressing the land problem and the connection between congestion, bad tenements and speculation in land. Mr. de Forrest looked at me with the maddening tolerance of a wise old man for a well-intentioned young fool and said, "If you touch the land problem in New York, you probably won't last here two years."

His tone and demeanor seemed to wish me less than luck, and I couldn't really blame him, because there was I, a newcomer upstart, and from Philadelphia of all places, who was challenging the sages of tenement house reform and telling them they weren't being practical. I told him I should keep right on stressing the importance of the land problem.

Jacob Riis backed the Congestion Committee in our fight against land speculation, and spoke for us frequently, and Florence Kelley in her incisive way said publicly, "A great trouble with housing reformers has been that they ignore the land problem entirely."

I stayed in New York ten years after Mr. de Forrest's dire prediction, always fighting land speculation and land speculators. To be sure it was often by the skin of my teeth, but I had several times as many teeth then as more recently.

My encounter with J. P. Morgan was brief, and resulted only in a continuation of his having his opinion of me and I having mine of him. Through a friend, the great financier agreed to give me five minutes. I met him in his little private office in the big building at the corner of Broad and Wall Streets in New York. He was sitting as I was ushered in, and asked what I wanted. I told him we wanted him to contribute to help our efforts to improve the condition of the people in the tenements, and outlined how.

"Young man," he said (this was over forty years ago), rising from his chair, "I've always been more interested in improving my own condition than that of other people."

"Mr. Morgan," I shot back as he walked toward the door into another office, "I've always understood that to be the case." He looked furious, but didn't turn back. I sensed the interview was ended, and left enriched in experience and out of pocket only two carfares.

I fared better with Andrew Carnegie. When I was admitted to the study in his wonderful mansion on Fifth Avenue, I found Dr. Harry R. Garfield, at the time President of Williams College, bent on the same errand, but in larger denominations.

"I thought you two gentlemen would be as interested in what each other is doing, as I am in what both of you are doing," Mr. Carnegie said, to set us at ease.

Mr. Garfield talked for a few minutes, and then Mr. Carnegie asked me to explain what the Congestion Committee was doing. It was late afternoon, and I thought Mr. Carnegie looked a little drowsy as he turned to me, and within ten minutes he was sound asleep. Dr. Garfield and I looked at each other, and I decided to keep on talking, but raised my voice and in a few minutes Mr. Carnegie looked up, as keen as ever, and said to me, "That is very interesting."

I knew it was best for me to leave while that feeling prevailed, and bidding him farewell, I deserted Dr. Garfield, or should I say left him a free field!

A few days later we got a check for $250 from Mr. Carnegie's office. I could never quite figure out whether the gift was Mr. Carnegie's apology for going to sleep while I was talking, or in appreciation of our work; but as it was never renewed, I incline to the view it was a sop to his conscience for his unintentional discourtesy in succumbing to the soporific qualities of my voice.

I never learned how much, if any, Dr. Garfield got.

CHAPTER THREE

Approaching War to End War

IN THE EARLY SUMMER of 1912 the Reform Club, dedicated to lower tariffs and ultimate free trade, of which Theodore Roosevelt was at one time a member, asked me to make an investigation and prepare a report on the need for lowering tariffs. It was expected that the Democrats in their campaign that year, under the leadership of Woodrow Wilson, would revert to their first principles, so I got leave of absence from the Congestion Committee and started investigations. The Club issued a series of bulletins, for most of which I prepared the material.

In the early fall the Democratic National Committee, which had headquarters in New York, asked me to write much of its text book material on the tariff and to organize exhibits showing the need for lower tariffs. I agreed to do so, but with the definite pledge that no local candidates nominated by Tammany Hall or by Democratic machines in any of the cities where the exhibits were held should be allowed to speak at meetings in the exhibits.

Among the important Democrats in charge at the headquarters were William G. McAdoo, later Secretary of the Treasury, William C. Redfield, later Secretary of Commerce, Josephus Daniels, later Secretary of the Navy, and Abram Elkus, who was in immediate charge of the exhibits, and Henry Morgenthau, Treasurer of the Democratic National Committee, both of whom were destined to receive recognition of their services, through appointment as Ambassador to the Sublime Porte at Constantinople.

Among the exhibits were a three-room furnished apartment, with a tag on every article of furnishing, including bedding, and on foods, showing how much more people paid for these articles because of a tariff. There were the regular charts, diagrams, etc., showing the double price system—what manufacturers charged domestic consumers and how much cheaper they sold these products abroad. It was called "dumping" in those days.

We got called by the Colgate Company on one slight inaccuracy, but this was the only instance of any comeback.

Things went along all right and we had exhibits in Chicago, Philadelphia and Boston, as well as New York.

About the middle of October Tammany Hall got uppish and insisted upon having local candidates speak at the noonday meetings in our exhibit on Union Square in New York, including William Sulzer, the Democratic candidate for Governor. I protested to the whole Democratic Committee, and the immediate sponsors of my work admitted that they had agreed to my stipulation that no Tammany candidate should be allowed to capitalize on the exhibit, but Tammany was obdurate and insisted. Strongly as I supported

Woodrow Wilson, I equally opposed Tammany Hall; and I handed in my resignation.

Every one of the prominent gentlemen I have mentioned expressed personally their appreciation for the work I had done; but of course they couldn't afford to alienate Tammany or Tammany votes. Mr. Elkus asked me to stay on until the end of the campaign, offering to pay my salary personally, because he said he did not trust the Democratic "patriots" who were working in the various exhibits and was afraid they would steal all the material (including the household furnishings, much of which we had rented) before the election. I declined to let him pay my salary, but stayed on as a volunteer.

Immediately after the election that year, I went to Europe for a syndicate of papers, of which Henry J. Wright, manager of the old *New York Evening Globe,* was director, to report on the economic background of the first Balkan war.

My work was facilitated by the wide acquaintance my father had with political leaders in Bulgaria. On my way to that country I interviewed some leaders in London, then went to conferences with Prime Ministers Pasitch of Servia in Belgrade, and Gueshov of Bulgaria in Sofia. These were in late November, by which time the four Balkan allies had driven the Turks out of Macedonia and the Servians and the Bulgarians were investing Adrianople.

Mr. Pasitch gave me the first intimation that there was any break between his and the Bulgarian government, tracing for me on a map the areas which the various Balkan allies had agreed to take, after driving the Turks out of Macedonia. He claimed the Servians were entitled to more, because they had used more troops. This was true, but it was equally true that the Bulgarians were much more efficient.

I stopped a day at my parents' home at Philippopolis, to get permission to go to Adrianople, which was under siege by Servian infantry and Bulgarian artillery. Reverend Woodruff, a young colleague of my father, went with me.

The military train on which we had transportation reached Mustapha Pasha, about twelve miles from the Bulgarian artillery investing Adrianople, around midnight. No hotel (khan) was open, so we went into a deserted building in the outskirts of the little place, which we found open. Mr. Woodruff lay on a bench and I threw myself on a pile of straw in a common room. The next morning we learned it was a deserted pest house!

That night in a little wine house, we ran into Colonel Frederick Palmer, the famous war reporter, and Robert Hare, world-known war photographer. They had been trying for days to get permission to go to the front, but were unable to do so, nor did our interceding the next morning help them.

Mr. Woodruff and I were unable to get transportation, so we hiked the eleven miles down the railroad track to the headquarters of the Servian command, and were bunked in straw on the floor, and had mess with young Servian officers, two of whom had been in New York on business. The following day we got to the batteries investing the city, but there was a day's truce and things were very quiet.

I was under contract to report the conference in London between Turkey and the Balkan allies, starting December 14, but stopped on my way back to call on the two Premiers I had seen on my way down. When I got off the train at Budapest to change cars, I noted a man following me, but I stepped outside the station proper to get some Hungarian money and was immediately arrested by a gendarme, who took me to the Station Master. This official, after agreeing my passport was in perfect order, insisted upon seeing all my documents and also examining my baggage, which of course had been done at the border. In an inner-pocket I had the map which Premier Pasitch had traced for me, and several films of the batteries, etc., near Adrianople, which I refused to show, and demanded instead that I be released. Had it not been for my contract, I would have stayed arrested and made a grand story of it; but I finally prevailed on the Red-Taper to let me go, and just caught the train.

My first cable to my syndicate of papers from London carried the statement that the Balkan conference with Turkey was only the tail of the kite, and that the real kite was the conference of Ambassadors of the Five Great Powers which immediately preceded the show conference. The conference of the Balkan allies and the Turks was reportedly financed by Baron de Hirsch, an international financier with a finger in every European pie.

Europe was not as interesting to Americans in 1912 as today, and I got a good many scoops—from my friends in the Bulgarian Delegation, through my acquaintance with Mr. Pasitch, and through an introduction to Dr. Streit of the Greek Delegation from my friend Professor J. Irving Manatt, a Grinnell College alumnus, formerly American Consul at Athens, who was in London at the time.

During this conference I had two interviews with M. Venezilos, Premier of Greece, and asked him about a matter which was even then creating trouble between Bulgaria and Greece and which rankles to this day. The Greek and Bulgarian armies had reached Salonika and, upon the surrender of that city, both armies on different sides agreed to march in together the next morning, and occupy the city jointly,

Instead, the night before, the Greek army went in and stole the show, and also the city. The Bulgarians suggested a plebiscite to determine to which country that famous and important seaport should go. The Greeks refused it.

In answer to my question as to why the Greeks refused this vote to let the citizens of Salonika determine their future, M. Venezilos replied that there were more Bulgarians in Salonika than Greeks and that "the Jews" were more friendly to the Bulgarians than to the Greeks! I also had several conferences and got much help from Dr. E. J. Dillon, expert on world affairs.

Nothing important came of the conference—except sowing the seeds for the second Balkan war and for World War I.

The "Ludlow Massacre" of men, women and children in Colorado, during the strike against the Colorado Fuel & Iron Co., had aroused the nation almost as much as the Triangle Shirtwaist Co. fire in New York City in 1911, when over a hundred girls lost their lives or were brutally burned because exits were locked.

"Mother" Jones, idol of coal miners, as John Mitchel had been a decade before, came East to tell the story and offset the publicity of Ivy Lee to whitewash the Company and the Rockefeller interests which controlled it. I organized a well-packed meeting in New York early in 1913, at which "Mother" Jones captured the audience, and Senator James E. Martine, Democrat of New Jersey, explained the bill he had introduced to have the Government take over the coal mines. Later I backed this bill at hearings in Washington.

Late in December of 1916 I married; and have two children, Michael and Ursula.

By January 1917 the wardogs were baying at full strength. I worked with the National Emergency Peace Committee in New York, with which many prominent peace workers were identified. Early in the year we held a mass meeting in Carnegie Hall, with outstanding speakers, where I made a successful appeal for funds to send "Twelve Apostles" over the country to demand that the Democrats keep their pledge and keep us out of war.

Just before this, the forces seeking to save Britain had organized a huge meeting in the old Madison Square Garden, with Professor Franklin H. Giddings of Columbia, President Patten of Princeton University and General Leonard Wood, as main speakers. The Garden was packed, and demands for conscription of American boys, for construction of armaments and for turning our country over to defend the Allied cause were fervent and loudly applauded. A lot of money was represented in that audience.

I rose and started to read a resolution that if we conscripted the boys of the Nation to fight the war we should conscript the wealth of the Nation to pay for it. It produced results. Within two minutes, three or four of the 2,000 men in uniform, whom Police Commissioner Arthur Woods had organized, were on my back or at my side; and I was hustled out to an ante-room and frisked. These toy soldiers did not find anything on me, but one of them socked me on the chin and then in the back of my neck. A plainclothes detective advised me to beat it before I was killed, and escorted me to a street car; so, as he said, "You will have a chance to get home alive."

Two nights later at a similar mass meeting in the Garden, after my doctor had fixed me up, I was one of several speakers who demanded conscription of money as well as men. The *New York Times* and the *New York World* reported I had asked the audience to pray for the death of Root and Roosevelt (T. R.). My advance copy didn't carry that statement, and I didn't make it. The *World* carried my denial, the *New York Times* ignored it, and two or three days later, the *World* had an editorial entitled, "Watch the Clock, Mr. Marsh." I wrote them I was watching it.

Two days after the meeting the Treasurer of the Lower Rents Society wrote in his resignation. I went to see him and asked if his action had anything to do with the fact that he was Counsel for the British-controlled Cunard Steamship Co., at a reported salary of $15,000. He denied it with vigor and strong language, but he stayed resigned. So did I, knowing that coming events usually cast their shadows before.

Just a few days before the Congress of the United States declared that a state of war existed with the Imperial German Government, I addressed a meeting in Baltimore's Music Hall, with the late David Starr Jordan, President of Leland Stanford University. The Chairman was Dr. Richard W. Hogue, a Baltimore clergyman. I had made my talk, in which I charged that certain banking interests friendly to the British Government, and which had made large loans to the British Government, wanted to take us into the war on the Allies' side, as they thought that was the only way to make their loans good. The audience, galleries included, agreed.

Dr. Jordan had just started his analysis of the international situation, when the outside doors (guarded by Baltimore's Chief of Police and a large squad of officers) were broken in, and scores of boys in uniform rushed up to the platform demanding—though somewhat bewildered by seeing the flag in full evidence—that the meeting be closed. The Chairman tried to quiet them, and asked them to retire.

As they clambered over the front of the platform, I suggested to Dr. Jordan that as there were plenty of huskies on the platform and in the audience we should help the police suppress the riot. He told me that theoretically I was correct, but practically it would be unwise. His judgment was admirable.

Some years after the war, Dr. Hogue told me that a few days after this incident the Chief of Police of Baltimore came to him and told him that he had thought that man Marsh was talking through his hat when he charged that the bankers were interested in the war, but that he had changed his mind the morning after our meeting, when he was called on the carpet by the higher-ups of the City Administration because he had cracked one of the ringleaders, in uniform, who was breaking up the meeting and this ringleader turned out to be the son of one of Baltimore's most prominent and most patriotic bankers!

A few days before Congress made its declaration that a state of war existed, hundreds of people from many states in sympathy with the Emergency Peace Committee met in Washington in an attempt to dissuade their members of the Senate and the House from voting for such a declaration. The tenseness was terrific; and the mass meeting, held in the old Convention Hall at 5th and K Sts., N.W., was frequently interrupted by jeers and cat-calls from the audience, while hundreds of boys in uniform milled around outside the Hall, threatening maximum violence to the "damned pacifists" who wanted their country invaded or were "pro-German."

After the state of war was declared, things were pretty tough for pacifists and for those who realize war is never a solution. The New York papers had ridden me a good deal. But I was still at large and attempting to organize a movement to get America to pay for the war as we went.

In August of that year, Mr. Arthur LeSueur, counsel for the National Non-Partisan League, of which A. C. Townley was the aggressive president, planned a big farmers' convention in St. Paul for September, to assure the Government that the farmers of the Northwest were backing the war but did not want war profiteers to use it to make a killing. The League asked me to come up to St. Paul, help organize the conference and handle the publicity; and I accepted.

At the time the leaders of the League were drafting a national platform for the League; and they included a plank favoring the transfer of taxes on buildings to land values, as well as one for profitless defense (though otherwise phrased) and for drastic taxation of incomes, and much public ownership.

Senator William E. Borah addressed the convention, which jammed Convention Hall, and denounced the war profiteers as few could do.

Senator Robert M. LaFollette was scheduled to make a leading address at the evening mass meeting. I was unable to get a copy of the address, or even to find out what stenographic service was preparing it, until about six o'clock on the evening of the talk. A hasty reading of it convinced me that it was very loaded for that audience of farmers. I knew that the reactionaries in Minnesota, particularly in the Twin Cities, and the Department of Justice, were hot on the trail of the League; so I showed it at once to Mr. Townley, Mr. LeSueur, and William B. Colver, then Federal Trade Commissioner. They all agreed with me, and Messrs. Townley and Colver went to Senator LaFollette's hotel to urge him not to make the speech, while I sat on the copies of his proposed speech sent over to the Hall, so the newspapermen could not get them. They were jolly mad.

I was told that evening that Senator LaFollette was much

chagrined and wanted to get out of making any speech; but his wife, always level headed, prevailed upon him to deliver one of his Chautauqua addresses, dealing with America's general problems. He was getting along all right with this speech, when he was interrupted by some heckler to whom he responded, "We *have* a grievance against the German Government." The Associated Press sent out the untruthful charge that he had said, "We have *no* grievance against the German Government."

The fat was in the fire the next morning.

Four Years Lobbying for Farmers

On the first of March, 1918, I started my first Washington job as editor of the *Farmers Open Forum,* and Secretary and Director of Legislation of the Farmers National Council, of which George P. Hampton was Managing Director. This Council was a very loose organization, which included at times the National Non-Partisan League, the American Society of Equity, the Washington State Grange and the State Farmers Unions of North Carolina and Nebraska. Although the state organizations mentioned were affiliated with their national organizations, they were far ahead of them on economics.

The *Farmers Open Forum* had a circulation of about 40,000 and was running a debate on public ownership of telephones. Nearly three quarters of the circulation was paid for at wholesale rates by the American Telegraph and Telephone Company, which also advertised in the magazine. The conclusion, by Mr. Hampton, was favorable to private owner-

49

ship of trunk lines and private or cooperative ownership of branch and local lines, but I editorially advocated public ownership of trunk lines, with cooperatives owning the rest.

The Honorable William Kent, former member of the House of Representatives from California, living at that time in Washington and a member of the U.S. Tariff Commission, was one of the most sincere backers and financial supporters of the Council. Another leader was Mr. Ed. C. Lasater of Falfurrias, Texas, where he had a ranch of 242,000 acres, but who frankly admitted the Nation would be better off if it ended private land monopoly. The President of the Council, Herbert F. Baker, a Republican State Senator in Michigan, lived on a farm in the Upper Peninsula.

The Council organized delegations of progressive farmers to the Capital and also presented their viewpoints on various measures affecting agriculture. My position was somewhat difficult, if not precarious. I knew pretty well several members of the Wilson War Cabinet: Secretary of the Treasury McAdoo; Secretary of War Baker; Josephus Daniels, Secretary of the Navy; W. B. Wilson, Secretary of Labor; William C. Redfield, Secretary of Commerce; and Franklin K. Lane, Secretary of the Interior. I had met David F. Houston, Secretary of Agriculture; Albert S. Burleson, Postmaster General; and Attorney General A. Mitchell Palmer. Louis F. Post, Assistant Secretary of Labor, I had known well for a decade.

My position on the war was fairly well known, for I had earned the characterization of "Champion Irritant" and had for years been getting wide publicity in New York papers, as well as a good deal over the country. I realized that the Department of Justice, or at least the Criminal Investigation Section, in which J. Edgar Hoover was even then a big shot, probably had my name on their list of "undesirables"; and I knew that the slightest lapse from patriotic discretion might deprive me of that pursuit of life, liberty, and happiness to which I had been addicted.

During the first months of my war year in Washington, I saw several of the members of the Cabinet I have mentioned, usually with Mr. Hampton, and on matters affecting farmers and taxation, for our people were very keen on paying for the war as it went. I also asked most members of the Cabinet mentioned to write a special article in their field for the *Farmers Open Forum,* and also certain Congressional leaders, like Champ Clark, Speaker of the House. When I asked the Speaker for an article, mentioning the members of the Cabinet who had agreed to write one, he snorted: "If they were not members of the Cabinet nobody would read what most of them write." Most members of the Cabinet were cordial, for they knew, as I did, that I had not committed any overt act.

In the spring of that year we created the Farmers National Committee on War Finance, of which Governor Arthur Capper of Kansas (later Republican U.S. Senator) was Chairman, which compiled data showing how the war could be financed out of current taxation. When I appeared before the House Ways and Means Committee on the Revenue Bill, I suggested that I was willing to have the Committee double the tax rate on my income if they would do that also on the incomes of Rockefeller and Morgan. Claude Kitchen of North Carolina, Chairman, asked me to repeat that statement, and then remarked, for the record, "You are perfectly safe in making that offer, because they will never double the tax rate on the Rockefellers and Morgans. They are not going to pay for the war that way."

At this hearing Congressman J. Hampton Moore, former Republican Mayor of Philadelphia, made a desperate effort to trap me into denouncing the war, after he had vigorously opposed my suggestion that we pay for it currently. I called attention in the hearing to the fact that members of Congress had evidently forgotten that they were American citizens, since they had failed to tax themselves. This suggestion to the Ways and Means Committee, and my offer to pay more taxes, provided me with a much needed alibi on my opposition to our entering the war.

That spring, with American soldiers going in large numbers to Europe, brought renewals of anti-Red drives and an effort by the Government or members of Congress to tie the tag of disloyalty to everyone who suggested that it was a profiteers' war. Under some pretext A. C. Townley, President of the Non-Partisan League, was brought to Washington by a Senate Committee in the early spring, to be questioned on the position of the League on the war. He was clearly rattled and made somewhat evasive answers, but was let off with a warning.

Mr. William F. Cochran of Baltimore, who was in charge of educational work of the Y.M.C.A. in the training camps, asked me if I would go to Camp Meade, some twenty miles from Washington, one or two nights a week, to talk to the soldiers in training. I asked him what I should talk about, and he replied, "Tell them what they will get when they come back from winning the war to make the world safe for democracy." I assured him that if I told them the truth about that, they would not go to the war and I would go to jail. So we compromised, and I talked on what they had the right to expect when they came back from the war, in the way of a different economic system under which they would have security and employment at fair wages. They were very attentive and asked highly intelligent questions.

That spring the crisis developed on wheat. The Farmers National Council called a wheat conference with delegates from Kansas, Nebraska, Oklahoma, Oregon, Washington, and North Dakota, which demanded a minimum of $3.00 a bushel. Figures presented on costs of production gave apparent justification for the figure—wheat had sold as high as $3.50. Wheat growers were much opposed to the final figure recommended, and adopted, of $2.20 a bushel; and blamed labor for fixing this price.

In June of that year, Mr. Hampton went as was his custom to the convention of the Washington State Grange, whose Master William Bouck was a stormy petrel in that state as A. C. Townley was in the Middle Northwest. The meeting was held in a most conservative town, Walla Walla; and it was broken up by the super patriots of that area, who disliked the radicalism of Mr. Bouck and charged that he was disloyal. The charge was promptly investigated by the Department of Justice, acting through Mr. John Lord O'Brian, and he was completely exonerated.

In July 1918 the Federal Trade Commission, which had conducted an investigation of the meat packing industry for several years, published its reports and recommendations. The Trade Commission, created in the early days of the Wilson Administration, was then highly progressive, with Wm. B. Colver and Victor Murdock, Democrats, and James E. Fort, Republican, as Commissioners. They made startling revelations of monopoly, vicious trade practices and profiteering.

One of the most dramatic incidents in the Commission's report was the story of the "Black Book" kept by one of the big meat concerns, in which false figures were entered and a fake set of books kept to mislead the public as to the profits of the concerns. The Commission showed that the Big Five meatpackers were interested in some 500 different kinds of foods in addition to their regular meat business. It recommended that the Federal Government take over main plants, warehouses, branches, railway sidings and tracks owned by the meatpackers—chiefly the Big Five (at that time Armour, Morris, Wilson, Cudahy, and Swift).

These recommendations aroused the usual howl from the meatpackers, for some had admitted they "faced prosecutions" when organized thievery was exposed. The first step they took was to try to come to some compromise through the entering of a Consent Decree, which was accomplished that fall. The meatpackers agreed to desist from all unfair trade practices and within a short time to divest themselves of all unrelated lines of business. As a matter of fact, they failed to comply with the terms of the Consent Decree and tried furtively and repeatedly to have the Consent Decree set aside, up till the enactment of the Packers and Stockyards Act of 1921.

The Farmers National Council had to be constantly on the alert to prevent this. John Fitzpatrick, President of the Chicago Federation of Labor, who had always made a big fight for workers in the packing industry in Chicago and elsewhere, saw President Wilson about the situation and got assurance from him that unless the meatpackers changed their tactics, paid fair wages and stopped profiteering, he would use the emergency war powers vested in him and take over the meatpacking business. We repeatedly reminded the President that the meatpackers had not complied with decent standards, and urged him to carry out this pledge, but without avail.

During the summer of 1918, Dr. William J. Spillman, who had been at the head of the office of farm management in the Department of Agriculture for nearly sixteen years, had a run-in with Secretary of Agriculture Houston which greatly stirred the farmers of the country. Dr. Spillman had developed a system of ascertaining costs of production, to which Secretary Houston was opposed, since he was still of the school which holds that the farmer's chief end is to make two blades of grass grow where one grew before, regardless of what effect it had on the farmer. Dr. Spillman told the story of the effort of the General Education Board to control the educational institutions of the North, as they had controlled those of the South. At that time the Rockefeller interests, through the General Education Board, were contributing to the Department of Agriculture.

Shortly after Mr. Houston became Secretary of Agriculture, the Bureau of Rural Work was started, and Professor Thomas Nixon Carver of Harvard was selected as head. He outlined an investigation to be conducted by his Bureau, covering economic conditions among farmers, costs of production and methods of distribution of farm products. Within a few days, Dr. Buttrick, then Secretary of the General Education Board, came to Washington and called Professor Carver down for making public his statement on the economics of the farm situation. Dr. Carver ordered Dr. Buttrick out of his office but he himself was forced to resign, and returned to Harvard.

Mr. Kent, whose family had long been in the livestock business, and Mr. Lasater, also a large cattle grower, had a running fight, in which the Farmers National Council cooperated, with Mr. Herbert Hoover, as Food Administrator. Time after time Mr. Hoover, who failed to establish any effective control over the meatpackers or their prices, put some restrictions on the livestock growers and failed to back them in their efforts to get minimum costs of production and to break the control of the meatpackers over livestock growing. On March 16, 1918, Mr. Kent, on the letterhead of the U.S. Tariff Commission, wrote President Wilson: "As a matter of fact, there is among livestock people a lack of confidence in the Government's policy or absence of policy, which, coupled with serious losses due to stimulated output, and curtailed demand, will without question result in a disastrous diminution of meat supplies, unless there shall be a change."

In the late summer of 1918, a war revenue bill was introduced which failed to meet any of the tests for a decent war tax bill. I saw President Wilson alone at the White House on this bill, and told him it was a "shark's" bill. He admitted it was a little "sharky," but said, "People won't stand for a real tax measure." I replied, "You are President, and you can insist on a decent bill if you want to." He had the grace to flush a bit, and for fifteen or twenty minutes we discussed the war and what the outcome would be. He was not as optimistic as his public statements on the war and particularly his reply to the Pope's peace note indicated, and I went beyond formal propriety in giving my opinion of the war, which he took in good part.

Armistice Day in the National Capital produced mixed feelings: relief that hostilities were ended; and, almost equally and naturally, fear on the part of many Government workers that the end of the war meant the end of their jobs in Washington—as it did. The great demobilization of Government workers in Washington started soon. Probably President Wilson's appeal in October for a Democratic Congress was one of the most serious political mistakes he made, and the resultant overwhelmingly Republican House elected that fall was a response to his mixing partisan politics with international affairs.

The months following the Armistice were anxious ones in Washington. The White House was swamped with suggestions as to resettlement projects for the demobilized army and for Government controls over industry. Farmers objected to the proposed sale of food surpluses at less than current prices. It was President Wilson's insistence that he control and determine America's part in the Peace Conference and peace terms which engendered extreme bitterness among Republicans, and some Democrats, in both branches of Congress.

Among the suggestions made in the early post-war years was that farmers curtail their acreage and production as advocated later by the "New Deal." This was urged by Republican Secretary of Agriculture Henry C. Wallace in 1921, just as vigorously as it was a dozen years later by his Democratic son, Henry A. Wallace, Secretary of Agriculture under President Roosevelt. Both of them knew most farmers are extreme individualists, as was inevitable in the early pioneering days, but which becomes disastrous in a maturing economy. So did George Norris, Chairman, after the Republicans took over in 1921, of the Senate Committee on Agriculture. He remarked to me that if he went to a wheat farmers' meeting at night and all those present agreed to reduce their acreage, he would get up early the next morning and start to increase it, because otherwise he would be the only farmer that didn't! Senator Norris also privately admitted we would have to come to large-scale farming, much of it run by cooperatives.

At my request in 1921 Sen. Norris appointed a Sub-Committee on Agriculture, of which Sen. Charles L. McNary of Oregon was Chairman, to study crop insurance, which the Farmers National Council was advocating. In my statement to this Committee, I stressed the fact that only Government could organize the financing of an inclusive crop insurance plan, or even insurance of major crops, but that such insurance would require Government to determine what and how much crops should be planted. A Government crop insurance plan was adopted a few years later, with a modicum of controls, but in January 1944 the U.S. Department of Agriculture Post-War Committee unanimously stated: "The agricultural production of the United States should be adjusted to national requirements, with due regard for export demand and desirable imports."

During the week that President Wilson spent in Washington on his visit from the Peace Conference, a group of farmers affiliated with the Farmers National Council, who had drafted a statement on peace terms, presented this to him in the White House and discussed the European situation with him. The statement reminded the world of the President's fourteen points, advocated more trade between countries, and a number of international controls. It contained the phrase, "There can be no peace between nations, until there is justice within nations." President Wilson looked through the statement and expressed his approval of every suggestion; but commented, with the utmost regret: "You gentlemen have very little comprehension of what I am up against at Versailles. I thought I should find much cooperation in trying to attain the objectives for which America entered the war, but I find that there is the same jealousy, rivalry, envy, and determination to extend the holdings of the Allies as after any war. Nearly everyone seems to want everything. The situation seems almost hopeless."

Mr. Charles S. Barrett, President of the National Farmers Union, had gone to Paris to follow the peace negotiations; and the Farmers National Council decided it would send three representatives for the same purpose, among them Dr. J. Weller Long, Secretary of the American Society of Equity, and Mr. Arthur LeSueur, Counsel for the National Non-Partisan League. The Administration had indicated its approval and we were daily expecting the passports, when Mr. Frank L. Polk, Acting Secretary of State, asked if Mr. LeSueur and I would come to his office at once. We did so, and he informed us that the British Government had objected to letting Mr. LeSueur go to Paris, on the alleged ground that the British Government had gotten hold of a letter Mr. LeSueur had written a dozen years before which he closed with the phrase "Yours for the revolution." This was customary Socialist signing off—the word "revolution" not implying any violence. Mr. LeSueur had been Socialist Mayor in Minot, North Dakota, years before, and as a lawyer had defended scores of members of the Industrial Workers of the World in their fight for economic justice and against persecution—and, incidently, had never lost a case. We had to accept the verdict of the Government—that is, of the British Government—and the trip was given up.

Nineteen-twenty was a year of extreme pessimism and depression. The glamour of the war was followed by complete disillusion as to what had been accomplished. The bitter fight in the Senate over America's participation in the League of Nations and adherence to the World Court reflected the feeling of the American people. In January of that year several farmers from northwestern states, who had attended the St. Louis Convention of the "Committee of 48," came to Washington to interview their Senators and see what could be done to get the program urged by that Committee adopted by Congress. This included higher taxation of incomes and of land values and public ownership of natural resources. Among the Senators they interviewed was Warren G. Harding of Ohio, destined to be selected by the Republicans as a compromise candidate for President that summer. The conversation turned to Russia, and Senator Harding said: "I have followed the Russian experiment with profound interest and sympathy, and I am forced to the conclusion that this Russian experiment will influence the world more profoundly than anything else since the birth of Christ." Events since then justify that conclusion.

The Federal Reserve Board was determined to deflate and try to get down to earth after the wild orgy of speculation in land stocks and commodities which had gone on since 1915. The Harding regime, when it came into power, adopted the policy. Farmers were furious, particularly those who should have known better than to pay up to $300 an acre for ordinary farm land, for which $50 would have been a fair price. Livestock growers of the Southwest were particularly hard hit. Mr. Lasater wired me from Texas to try to get, not a wiping-off of mortgage debt or a Government subsidy, but merely a slightly lower interest rate. I discussed the situation with members of both branches of Congress from agricultural States, and they agreed to back legislation refinancing farmers' short term debt at a lower rate of interest.

Fearing that Mr. Eugene Meyer, then Governor of the Federal Reserve Board, and Secretary of the Treasury Andrew W. Mellon would block this legislation, I called on Mr. Meyer and laid the situation before him, asking his help. He said he would not only not sanction lower interest rates, but would oppose such legislation. I told him I would go see the old man upstairs (Secretary Mellon in the Treasury Building). Mr. Meyer said he would beat me to it and, knowing the secret route through the building, he got in ahead of me so that when I reached the Secretary's ante-room I learned that Mr. Meyer was with him.

In a few minutes Mr. Meyer came out smiling and remarked to me that he had gummed the game for me. I assured him that I would ungum it somehow or other, and was ushered into the presence of the greatest Secretary of the

Treasury since his predecessor. Mr. Mellon justified the charge that he sweat ice water. I laid the situation before him, and asked him if he would not back legislation to give the livestock growers lower interest rates. He assured me he would not only not back such legislation but he would oppose it (Mr. Meyer's expression), and said: "Private bankers have plenty of money, they are perfectly willing to loan on good security at five to seven per cent. This is a field for private bankers and not for the Government." To my question as to whether private bankers would not charge "all the traffic will bear," Mr. Mellon replied: "Of course the bankers will charge all they can get. They are not in business for their health." I assured him the farmers were not in business for their health either, and conferred again with the members of both branches of Congress, who introduced legislation.

Two or three days later I went to see Secretary Mellon again and told him if he dared oppose the bill I would quote what he had told me about the bankers not being in business for their health. He agreed to keep quiet, and within a few days the bill providing a loan of about $25 million at fair interest rates became law. The Harding Administration did not quite dare continue the policy of sudden deflation of livestock prices through exorbitant interest rates, any more than did the Wilson Administration.

In the summer discontent grew so strong that important farm and labor groups with a scattering of "intelligentsia" forgathered in Chicago to organize a "Farmer-Labor Party." The meeting started out auspiciously with plenty of denunciations of existing conditions. Harmony stopped with the opening sessions. Among the leaders from the East were Amos Pinchot, J. A. H. Hopkins, and George L. Record of New Jersey. Delegates from the National Non-Partisan

League and from a few labor unions, chiefly from the Middle-West States, made up the bulk of the delegates, including Robert M. Buck, then editing a labor paper in Chicago. Warren S. Stone, President of the Brotherhood of Locomotive Engineers, was in the Great Northern Hotel in Chicago, watching events but unwilling to join the movement openly.

The night of the third day saw the beginning of the finish. The evening session lasted till two in the morning. With George Record in the Chair, Amos Pinchot tried to avert disaster. He finally said, "What is the reason you labor unionists and farmers won't cooperate in this movement?"

Robert Buck sprang to his feet and said: "The reason we don't want to tie up with you fellows from back East is that we don't trust you." My motion to adjourn until 9:00 the next morning prevailed. At that session the West's suspicions of the East flared so generally that hopes of a Farmer-Labor National Party in 1920 were killed beyond resurrection.

One of the big gains that had come out of the World War was the Government's taking over the telegraph companies and the Government control, under Director General Mc-Adoo, of the railroads. There was no Government operation. The same bunch of financial looters who had milked the railroads for half a century remained in control. The transportation Brotherhoods, known as the "Big Four," had backed the Plumb Plan for public ownership of the railroads with tri-partite control, one third representing stockholders, one third classified employees, and one third official employees. They formed the "Plumb Plan League" and campaigned the country. President Stone of the Locomotive Engineers was most active.

During the late months of 1920 presidents of the railway men's organizations, who were anxious to have Government control of railroads continue, had collected affidavits from conductors, firemen, mechanics, electrical workers, telegraphers, dispatchers, etc., as to the sabotage which even during the war some of the financial interests had conducted to discredit Government control; and turned them over to me. These I gave to several Senators, including LaFollette and Norris, under pledge of secrecy.

Railroad owners and management induced Senator A. B. Cummins of Iowa and Representative John J. Esch of Wisconsin, both of whom had been elected years before as "radicals" and opposed to the machinations of the railroads, to introduce the Cummins-Esch bill to return the railroads to private control and operation. Title had never passed from the owners to the Government; and, as Senator Cummins stated on the floor of the Senate when the bill to have the Government take over the roads was pending, the rental paid the railroads "shocked the moral sensibilities of mankind."

The election of Harding threw cold water on all progressives. In December I suggested to the executives of the railway men's organizations and to some of the farm organizations that we put on a campaign over the country to kill the Cummins-Esch railroad bill and try to continue Government control. They agreed, and I organized a series of conferences from New York to the Twin Cities in Minnesota, and Lincoln, Nebraska, to explain the situation. These were well attended. Mr. William H. Johnston, President of the International Association of Machinists, made the trip with me in connection with his official business as President of the union.

The most important meeting we had, though all the meetings were well attended, was in the Assembly Chamber of the Capitol in Madison, Wisconsin. I arranged for Senator LaFollette, who had not made a public appearance in Madi-

son since he was burnt in effigy there for his opposition to
the World War, to address the meeting. It was a dramatic
occasion. Every seat was taken half an hour before the meeting started, and not only the aisles but the corridors around
the Assembly Hall were jammed. The Senator made a quiet
but extraordinarily effective speech, referring only briefly to
the World War. He received an ovation at the beginning
and at the finish of his talk.

We did not succeed in defeating the Cummins-Esch railroad bill, despite the campaign, nor could we induce President Wilson to veto the bill. He was completely worn out,
and his faith in the processes of democracy had evidently
received a terrific blow.

Four incidents, in the hectic years following the winning
of the war to make the world safe for democracy, illustrate
the need for defining democracy.

Congress was considering a very vicious bill for leasing our
natural resources, sponsored in the Senate by the high priest
of "protection"—Reed Smoot of Utah and of the National
Association of Manufacturers. I had opposed it at a Public
Lands Committee hearing, and went to his office to plead
with him to modify at least some of the worst features. He
didn't deny any of my criticisms, but was obdurate. Finally
I asked him if it wasn't true that no Congress could bind a
succeeding one, and he agreed it was. "Then," I said to him,
"as soon as the people wake up, they can compel Congress to
take back what's left of their resources you are giving away,
without paying anything for them."

"Of course they can," he replied, "and that is the reason I
hope to God the American people never wake up." So far his
hope has not been dimmed, though the people have stirred
in their sleep.

While testifying before the Senate Committee on Finance, of which Boies Penrose of Pennsylvania was Chairman, I gave some startling, for those days, figures on the profits of corporations and big personal incomes, on both of which the tax was very low; and urged a sizable increase. When I went to correct my testimony, the universal practice, I found many of my figures stricken out, which meant they wouldn't appear in the printed record of the hearing. The clerk of the Committee explained the Chairman had ordered this and he had to comply—as of course he had to, or lose his job. Over the boy's protest, I stormed into Senator Penrose's private office and asked him by what authority he had tampered with my testimony.

"By my own," he replied, quite candidly.

"But this isn't legal, is it?" I put up to him.

The Harvard graduate—known as a reformer, chiefly of Philadelphia's municipal corruption, in his early post-college days—looked at me quizzically and with a perfectly refined Harvard accent, not sullied by long use in Philadelphia's vicious ward politics, replied: "Of course it isn't legal, but you can't do a damned thing about it."

That's where he was mistaken. I immediately gave a story to the newspapers, and got some publicity though no immediate redress. Republican leadership was encouraged by the nation's reaction to the slogan "back to normalcy" of its dark horse candidate, Warren G. Harding, whose selection was dictated by Senator Penrose from a sick-bed in Pennsylvania to the little operating clique in a smoke-filled room in the Blackstone Hotel, at the Chicago Republican Convention in 1920.

Henry Ford had two visions: the first getting the boys out of the trenches before Christmas 1917, via the Ford Peace Ship; the second having the Government sell him Muscle

Shoals for a song. His second vision almost came true, for
major industrial and farm and some labor organizations
backed his demand. The three most influential directors of
the Farmers National Council were from Michigan and
highly overawed by the genius of the man who for many
years didn't care what color his automobiles were so long as
they were black.

Ford claimed he wanted Muscle Shoals so he could furnish
farmers cheap fertilizer; I was convinced he was less concerned with fertilizing farms with cheap nitrates than with
fertilizing Ford profits with cheap power. I was also convinced that if the Government alienated any natural resource
it had developed, both conservation and public ownership
of natural resources would go out of the window for a long
long time. Probably I shocked my Board when as Director of
the Council I told them I wouldn't appear in favor of tariffs
on farm products, which a few favored; and then almost immediately refused to back the Ford offer. In my half-century
of lobbying, however, I have never advocated a measure I
didn't believe in personally, nor opposed one which I thought
meritorious. I am not qualified to state whether this was due
to principle or to obstinacy, but the line between them is
tenuous.

After considerable and by no means chilly argument, I
swung the Board, and was I believe the first witness to oppose the Ford offer before both Senate and House Committees. To his great credit, Dr. John A. Ryan (later Monsignor)
of the National Catholic Welfare Council, accepted our
invitation to urge these Congress Committees to hang on to
Muscle Shoals, and made a prophetic statement about the development of fascist controls through private monopoly of
natural resources. Had Ford gotten Muscle Shoals, I believe
the Rural Electrification program, Tennessee Valley Author-

ity, and extension of public power development as at Hoover Dam and Grand Coulee would have been long delayed and much harder to get. Ford's proposed grab could not have been defeated, probably, without the active support, as in every similar fight, of genuine progressive members of Congress such as Senators LaFollette, Norris, Ladd and Borah.

America's between-the-big-oceans position provides an additional source of paytriotism—from which land-locked and land-mass nations are immune—furnishing millions of tons of merchant ships for transport, often many thousands of miles, of millions of men and many millions of tons of supplies and war material. At the end of World War One these ships were a major prize, which "private enterprise" buccaneers were eager to grab. One of the big press organizations had a specialist study the shipping problem in 1920 for over a month, to oppose a bill pending in Congress to dispose of most of wartime-constructed ships and provide a subsidy to boot—or to booty.

This report couldn't appear, but the author asked me if I would take the material and boil it down to present to a joint hearing of the Senate and House Committees on the Merchant Marine. It was a masterly study. I agreed to do so, and the material was given me two days before the hearing, which was held in a Committee Room in the Capitol— jammed till there wasn't even standing room, chiefly with would-be beneficiaries, naturally hostile to me.

The statistical facts didn't seem to make much impression, while the appeal I made, "Don't give up the ships," was wasted on those who wanted the Government to do just that. Finally I dubbed the bill "An Ocean-Going Pork Barrel," and I could see by the faces of the proponents and fast working pencils of the reporters that I had struck legislative pay dirt. That stigma killed the bill—for the session.

The real reason? We are a nation of landlubbers—despite our propensity to ask Federal funds to deepen creeks, three hundred miles from the sea, to accommodate ocean craft—and if a pork barrel were ocean-going the pork wouldn't be available for home consumption! At an early session of Congress a big River and Harbors Bill—more pork barrels for the hinterland—was arranged, and there was no moaning at the crossroad bars to prevent one pork barrel from putting out to sea. The ship subsidy bill was passed!

CHAPTER FIVE

Working with Organized Labor

IT WAS CLEAR after the Harding election in 1920 that we were in for a black time and that farmers would probably be hardest hit of all. Senators LaFollette and Norris, with other progressives in both branches of Congress, organized in December that year the "People's Legislative Service," of which Basil M. Manley was Executive Director, to make investigations on legislative proposals and measures for the progressives in both branches of Congress.

Being convinced that investigations alone were not sufficient, and that an aggressive campaign for progressive measures was necessary to secure their enactment, I proposed to the executives of several railway men's organizations the creation of a "People's Reconstruction League," with a general membership, to work for a definite progressive program. They saw the force of this and agreed to form such an organization, with a program of farm aid, including control of

the meatpacking industry, progressive taxation, public ownership of the railroads and similar measures.

Hon. Herbert F. Baker as President of the Farmers Na-
tional Council, was elected President, and Mr. William H.
Johnston, President of the International Association of
Machinists, Vice-President, and I, Executive Secretary.
Among the officers of the League were Warren S. Stone,
President the Brotherhood of Locomotive Engineers, L. E.
Sheppard, President of the Order of Railway Conductors,
W. S. Carter, President of the Brotherhood of Railway Fire-
men and Enginemen, James P. Noonan, President of the
International Brotherhood of Electrical Workers, Martin F.
Ryan, President of the Order of Railway Carmen, and H. F.
Fljozdal, President of the Brotherhood of Maintenance of
Way Employees—the most poorly paid of all workers on the
railroads.

Three of the organizations for a few years contributed
$100 a month, one $50, and for a year one of them contributed some $200 a month, for the budget of the League.
They had appreciated the work I had done fighting the
Cummins-Esch Railroad Act, even if we did not succeed in
defeating it. I urged the sponsors to call the organization
"The People's Lobby," but they were afraid of the reaction
to the word "Lobby," as it had acquired with some justice a
rather sinister connotation. The organization of the League
was announced in January 1921, and we started appearing
before Committees of Congress on measures affecting our
program.

Several bills to control the meatpacking industry, based
upon the investigation by the Federal Trade Commission,
had been introduced in both branches of Congress but had
not had any success. The big meatpackers maintained a great
lobby here, "The American Institute of Meatpackers," well-

financed and fighting every effort to control this industry. The Senate Committee on Agriculture started long hearings, with Hon. Francis J. Heney, noted prosecution lawyer and former District Attorney of San Francisco, as counsel for a short time at the beginning.

Finally a somewhat obstinate Republican Norwegian from Mason City, Iowa, Representative Gilbert N. Haugen, Chairman of the House Committee on Agriculture, decided to hold his own hearings and draft a Packers and Stockyards Control Bill. He conducted hearings for several weeks at which scores of witnesses representing labor, farm, women's and consumers' organizations testified, while the meatpackers and their cohorts were given full opportunity to oppose the bill. The Committee gave me an opportunity to cross question all the meatpackers' witnesses—although some members of the Committee were very much opposed—and backed me up to the limit in compelling the packers' witnesses to answer my questions. It was, as far as I know, the only time that anyone but a lawyer had served in such a capacity.

Mr. Heney got a $1,000-a-week fee for his short but effective work, while I was getting $300 a month.

Out of the admissions and replies which the meatpackers' witnesses, including their highest-priced lawyers, made to my questions I built up the case for the House Committee's bill, which with amendments finally passed the Congress as the Packers and Stockyards Act of 1921.

We failed in our effort to get in the bill the recommendations made by the Federal Trade Commission in 1918 to have the Government take over warehouses, distributing agencies, and rail equipment of the meatpackers. The bill as finally adopted was, I think, the most important Government regulation of any major industry since the creation of the Interstate Commerce Commission in 1887. The administration was very faulty, however, because the packers were able to get their men into key positions. Three or four years later I made complaints against them and got Congressman Ed King of Illinois, Chairman of the House Committee on Expenditures in Executive Departments, to conduct an investigation, as a result of which two of the most prominent miscreants were promptly ousted—though they got other good Government jobs. But the effect was salutary.

In June 1921 Mr. Hampton, who had been in failing health for over a year, died on the eve of his visit to the Convention of the Washington State Grange. His wife, who had been his very able and devoted assistant, continued for a few months, till I was elected Director of the Farmers National Council while continuing as Secretary of the People's Reconstruction League.

In mid-summer of that year the Department of Justice, with the somewhat well known Harry M. Daugherty, Attorney General, sent an agent to our office to investigate me, apparently on the theory that I was getting Russian gold, although as a matter of fact I could not get enough American gold to make the old mare go very fast. As soon as the agent identified himself with his card signed by A. Mitchell Palmer —Attorney General under President Wilson—I sent for my secretary to take the interview down in shorthand. I opened the investigation of myself by turning to a list of the great lobbies operating in Washington, which Senator LaFollette had recently compiled, and asked the agent whether the Department of Justice was investigating the U.S. Chamber of Commerce, the American Institute of Meatpackers, the American Bankers Association, the Association of Railway Executives and about a dozen more. He finally insisted that he was investigating me, and not I him, and I had to admit that was the occasion for his visit, and answered all his questions truthfully and fully.

As soon as the notes were transcribed, I sent a copy of them to the Attorney General and asked him to give us a clean bill of health, telling him that he should be ashamed to waste the people's money investigating organizations trying to do the job for the people which he was being paid to do but was afraid to do. I also gave a copy of the transcript of the investigation to Senators LaFollette, Norris, and Ladd. When I saw Senator LaFollette about it, he remarked to me: "The Attorney General will always be more afraid of you than you have any reason to be afraid of him."

The Attorney General wrote me, in reply to my letter, that the Attorney General was not giving any help to publicity stunts.

Lest we forget, this was the Attorney General of Washington Court House, Ohio, fame, who was described by a Senator from Ohio, Mr. Willis, as "clean as a hound's tooth"; but who did not show up that way in the investigation that Senator Wheeler's and Senator Walsh's Committee made of the oil scandals and the little "Green House" on K Street.

In the spring of 1922 most of the Railway Men's Organizations, who were interested in both the People's Legislative Service and the People's Reconstruction League, with representatives from the general public and progressive farm organizations, decided to go in for non-partisan political action in a big way. They organized the "Conference for Progressive Political Action," of which William H. Johnston was chairman and Basil M. Manley secretary. This organization compiled the record of votes of most Senators and many members of the House of Representatives who were up for re-election, on not only labor measures but also measures affecting the general welfare. They organized State branches in several States and maintained a large office in Washington during the campaign, though most of their work was done by volunteers.

The Conference opposed in both the primaries and the final election a good many members of the House of Representatives, and a few Senators, whose voting record was against labor; and had to select candidates to run against them. The local or State Committees usually asked prospective candidates a lot of questions as to their economic beliefs. I urged them to find out first whether the candidate's wife had any social ambitions, and if so, not to endorse him, for I had learned that in Washington the *salon* had ruined many more progressives than the saloon.

At the request of the Conference, I spent about three months that summer campaigning in the Middle West and Far West, though without any salary from the Conference. The experience was highly illuminating.

Early in the year the railway-shopcrafts had taken a vote on a strike. I talked with most of their executives and warned them that farmers through these Western states, though thoroughly sympathetic with labor, were badly deflated and broke and would be unable to resist the temptation to take the jobs of the railway employees on strike, even though they gave free food to the strikers.

None of the "Big Four" of railway workers—the Engineers, Conductors, Firemen and Enginemen, and Trainmen—joined the strike; and I pled with Warren S. Stone, a very warm personal friend, to try to dissuade the men from striking. He did his best, as did most of the other executives of the railway men's organizations, but without success. Those workers, many of whom had seen service in France, really thought that the Government would make the railways squeeze the water out of their stock and meet major demands of their workers, most of which were very reasonable. They were wrong, and while the farmers in many states brought in carloads of food, drove in cattle on the hoof, and gave free milk, vegetables and fruits in season to the railroad strikers, enough farmers (though of course not always the same) took the jobs to break the strike.

Federal Judge Anderson of Indiana had issued an injunction restraining all concerned from giving any help of any sort whatever to the strikers, under severe penalties. This injunction was read in many of the strikers' meetings I attended in the West and Northwest and in the meetings of friendly farmers planning to supply food. It was greeted with yells of derision, as the plans for getting free food from the farmers and getting free bricks to throw at the strike-breakers were matured. It was need, and not the injunction, that broke the strike.

Among those for whom I campaigned that summer were Burton K. Wheeler in Montana, John B. Kendrick in Wyoming, Robert M. LaFollette in Wisconsin, and Henrik Shipstead in Minnesota. While I was speaking at a meeting in the primary in Montana, a quiet intellectual-looking man came in and listened attentively to what I had to say. He was introduced, as soon as I got through, as the Democratic candidate, Mr. Wheeler. Although Wheeler had never been in either branch of Congress, he had endeared himself to the progressives not only of Montana but of the nation for the courageous way in which, as Federal Prosecutor in Montana during the orgy of war patriotism, he had defended the I.W.W., labor leaders, and all citizens in their civil liberties. He also had an enviable record of fighting the twin rulers of the State, the Montana Power Company and the Anaconda Copper Company. I traveled with him in the primary a few

days, and for several days in the finals. He was handsomely
elected.

Senator John B. Kendrick was up for re-election, after
many years in the upper branch at Washington, and in campaigning for him I traveled with his current secretary, Joseph
C. O'Mahoney, who on the Senator's death was appointed to
the unexpired term and served in the Senate many years,
despite his fight against President Roosevelt's Supreme Court
plan. He was Chairman of the Temporary National Economic Committee, which was (unfortunately) too long on
statistics and short on basic conclusions on economic issues.

Senator Shipstead was running as a Farmer-Laborite, but
the burden of our talks in the nine days I spent in that campaign was that we should defeat the incumbent Frank B.
Kellogg, who had a bloated reputation as "Trust Buster,"
chiefly brag. We nicknamed him "Nervous Nelly."

In all the States in which I campaigned for members of the
House of Representatives as well as Senators, but particularly in Minnesota, Montana, Wisconsin and Washington,
the biggest issue was the involvement in the World War and
the results. This was of course notably so in Wisconsin. The
Washington office of the Conference was sure that LaFollette
would be elected. But his son Robert (later successor to his
father) wired me while I was on the Pacific Coast, begging
me to come there for a week. Senator LaFollette's stock was
rising rapidly in Wisconsin, as was proven in the reception
he got in February 1921, at the meeting referred to earlier,
in the Legislative Hall in Madison. There seemed little opposition to him and he came through with a thumping majority. He had a wonderful political machine of a high order,
a splendid record, and two remarkable sons—a combination
highly useful in a political campaign.

In Washington State the contest was extremely bitter. The

Republican incumbent, Senator Miles C. Poindexter, had been elected in 1912 on the Bull Moose ticket, but had gone reactionary. In 1921, long before the birth of the American Liberty League, he had introduced a bill making striking a felony. The progressive forces, state and national, had endorsed for their candidate in the Republican primary against Poindexter, Mrs. Silas B. Axtell, whose husband was a prominent physician in Bellingham. In the Democratic primary they endorsed Clarence C. Dill, who had been defeated when he ran for Representative after voting against America's declaration of war. He was anxious to stage a comeback vindication, and succeeded. It was quite obvious that Mrs. Axtell, the first woman to run for the U.S. Senate, could not be elected, even in as progressive a State as Washington. We chopped the Republican vote to pieces, however, and that let Mr. Dill get in—since a large part of the votes that went to the three contenders against Poindexter in the Republican primary went to Dill in the election.

The Conference had adopted a moderate program on taxation, public ownership of the railroads and the meatpacking industry, labor legislation, and aid to farmers. A large proportion of the people endorsed by the national and state Conferences for Political Action were elected; and in late November of that year the Conference held a meeting of jubilation in Cleveland. Some of the delegates seemed to think that they had the political world by the tail and it was time to start a labor party. The Conference had been non-partisan, backing candidates on their record, regardless of party affiliation. A large proportion of the delegates at Cleveland wished to continue this policy. Mr. Sidney Hillman, President of the Amalgamated Clothing Workers, insisted that the Conference should organize itself into a new political party, asserting that labor had no future as a tail to

either of the two old parties. Most of the unions in the
A.F. of L. were opposed to independent political action and
the "Big Four" transportation workers were highly luke-
warm, so no decision was reached.

An incident during the campaign in the office of Governor
Hunt of Arizona, in Phoenix, was illuminating on the ethi-
cal basis of politics. The Governor, with whom I had been
discussing the political situation, had left the room; and
while I was talking with the Democratic leader of the State
I asked him what the people of Arizona thought about Secretary Fall getting the $100,000 in a little black bag, for back-
ing certain oil grants. Secretary Fall had lived many years in
Arizona and had played poker to the tune of thousands of
dollars, plus or minus, a good many nights. This peerless
Democrat looked me straight in the face and said: "We
think he was a . . . ., he ought to have taken at least a million dollars and passed some of it around out here. We need
it."

Shortly after Harding's inauguration, an experience with
Herbert Hoover, Secretary of Commerce, was equally revealing. The Russian famine was about at its height. The reports
of suffering and starvation were appalling; and Members of
Congress, shocked by the tragedy, introduced a resolution to
have the Federal Government appropriate $20 million to
buy cereals, chiefly wheat, in America and send them to Russia. There was a report that Mr. Hoover was opposed to this;
but, knowing the prominent part he had taken in relief in
Belgium and other sections of Europe, I felt he must have
been maligned. So I went to see him and laid the case before
him.

He listened attentively, then smashed his fist on the top of
his desk and said: "Marsh, the height of my ambition is to

crush out the Soviet form of Government and everything it represents."

"Do you mean you would let the children in Russia starve, to crush out the Soviet Union?" I asked.

"Yes, if necessary," he said.

I assured him he would not get away with it, and submitted his reply to the Senate Committee on Agriculture, of which George Norris was chairman, and before which the resolution was pending, asking that they invite Secretary Hoover to appear. They did so, and he replied with a blistering letter, but refused to come before the Committee. Within a few days the resolution passed Congress, the appropriation was made, and the food was on its way to Russia. No one thought of calling me a "communist" at that time—or since!

Things were rather slow in 1923. The Republicans were getting into full swing. Even then, however, Andrew Mellon was suggesting that, as the national income was increasing and Government tax receipts were going up, it would be wise to retire some of the war debt as it came due instead of refunding it. He was right, on that. This was opposed by a good many Democratic leaders, including Senator Pat Harrison and Representative John N. Garner of Texas.

The independent political movement got under full headway early in 1924, since it was quite obvious that the Democrats would nominate a conservative and that Calvin Coolidge, President through the death of Harding, would be the Republican nominee. The political conventions of the two old parties, with John W. Davis the Democratic candidate and Coolidge enthusiastically nominated by the Republicans, precipitated the convention in Cleveland in July at which Robert M. La Follette and Burton K. Wheeler were nominated for President and Vice-President on the Progressive ticket. I had the good fortune to be a member of the

Platform Committee at the Cleveland conference and again helped in getting a fairly progressive program.

That summer I spent several weeks campaigning for the ticket, particularly in the Middle West, and was more amused than shocked at the claims that the national office was making as to the election. Early in October I ventured the guess that the ticket would carry North Dakota and Wisconsin. I was correct, except as to North Dakota.

Two incidents in this campaign were rather significant. Mr. Rudolph Spreckles was manager of the La Follette campaign in California and organized a luncheon for me in San Francisco. Just before the luncheon he asked me whether, since there were reporters present, I would state that La Follette, if elected, would support tariffs on farm products to equal those on manufacturers. I assured him that if I thought Senator La Follette were going to do this I would not be supporting him, because it was quite clear to me that the tariff never helped farmers; but I added that, if they were on that tack in California, I would go out of the State without making a single speech, however much I should regret it. He was a good sport, and assured me that I should go ahead and make any speeches I wanted to. I did this, speaking in a good many farm centers, and ridiculed the idea that tariffs could be any help to farmers, suggesting that farmers stop speculating in land and end other speculations if they wanted to get ahead.

The other experience was in Dodge City, Kansas. The local chairman arranging my meeting was a barber. On my arrival late in the afternoon he remarked to me, taking me apart from the group, that he understood La Follette was coming out for the Ku Klux Klan, which he said would be very popular in Kansas. I again had to state that I would not be supporting La Follette if I thought he would be doing anything about the Klan except denouncing it.

Of course the result of the election was a bitter blow to some of the progressives, for they had already parcelled out the Cabinet jobs and most of the others paying $7,500 and up!

In 1925 the Garland Fund had made an appropriation of about $3,000 to enable the People's Reconstruction League to extend its campaign against American imperialism. We had been opposing this vigorously, so much so that the Honorable Henry L. Stimson, then Secretary of State, complained to someone, "We get a plan all nicely laid for Central America, and that man Marsh comes along with a statement to the press and knocks it all out."

We had exposed, particularly, the manipulations of our State Department in Nicaragua and had attacked American fomenting of revolutions there. With the money from the Garland Fund we got out and widely circulated a pamphlet summarizing several books they had financed, including "American Bankers in Bolivia" and the story of American imperialism in Nicaragua, Cuba, Haiti, Puerto Rico and Santo Domingo. We called this "American Capitalism Abroad."

That summer Mr. Walter Liggett raised some funds and took Senator Lynn J. Frazier and me on a three-week speaking trip to the Coast, opposing American intervention in Mexico—using the example of what had happened in Nicaragua. Our meetings, usually sponsored by local groups and held in school houses, churches and labor temples, were well attended. In Portland, Senator Charles L. McNary was chairman and the large assembly hall in the Labor Temple was crowded. The press reported our meetings quite fairly.

While we were in Denver, President Coolidge came out

with his assertion that where the American dollar was there was American soil. At my instance, Senator Frazier issued at once a vigorous denunciation of this position, which the press carried well. The thing that really checked our intervention in Mexico, however, was an ultimatum Klan leaders gave Coolidge in the White House, that such action would bring political reprisals.

In December that year the People's Reconstruction League organized a conference for lower tariffs, held in the national capital, at which former Senator David I. Walsh of Massachusetts, who had been temporarily retired, made a vigorous attack upon protective tariffs. His experience reminded me that Senator Underwood told me, after his remarkable fight for lower tariffs and the enactment of the Underwood Tariff Bill in 1913, that he had received less than half a dozen letters from the entire United States thanking him for his efforts for the people! He was not critical, merely recording the facts.

During the summer of 1924 the Farm-Labor Union of the South requested me to represent them in Washington, even though the Farmers National Council was by that time only a paper organization. The organization was a bonafide farm organization, under responsible leadership, and had its books audited. It claimed at the time some 250,000 members. Its president W. W. Fitzwater, a farmer of Bonham, Texas, had been a Holiness minister, and carried over into his farm organization the technique which he used in purveying spiritual, instead of economic, salvation. Their headquarters was for a time in Dallas, Texas, and they published a weekly newspaper with E. R. Meitzen, a former editor of National Non-Partisan League papers, in charge, and I wrote a Washington letter for it.

During the summers of 1924 and 1925, I spoke at many

meetings and picnics for them (usually with Mr. Fitzwater), in Texas, Oklahoma, and Arkansas, with highly interesting experiences. The meetings were usually opened with singing and prayer, followed by exhortations to the farmers to stick together. In all these States the color line was drawn quite strictly. Negroes took the back seats, and at the picnics they waited until the white folks had eaten all they wanted before they came up to the tables, which were even then pretty well loaded with food.

Under the constitution of the organization, farmers agreed to market all their cotton through the organization's marketing branch. Unfortunately many of them were susceptible to the lure of one cent a pound more on cotton, their staple, and sold through local agents or cotton brokers, and this broke the organization within a few years. Some of the farmers planted part of the crop in the name of their wives or sons, so that they could evade the contract if they wanted to. Partly as a result of this experience, many farmers' selling cooperatives later adopted a binding contract with their members to sell all their cotton through the cooperative, with penalties for non-compliance.

A favorite illustration which Mr. Fitzwater used was to compare the condition of cotton farmers in war times and in the summers of 1924 and 1925. In war times, he said, when the farmer was going to drive to town for supplies he asked his wife what she wanted, and was able to buy them. In these later years, he said, all the cotton farmer could do was to inquire of his better half what she could "get by with."

One night in middle Texas I fell afoul of "chiggers," those invisible insects which burrow under the skin and produce torture almost equal to that of the famous bed-bug, but with the difference that you cannot have the satisfaction of seeing the "chiggers" and killing them. Strong soap was their un-

doing, and rubbing in salt helped. The next morning we had
to take a long ride to another meeting. I hadn't shaved, and
it was too hot to wear a tie. The chairman of our noon meeting looked at me skeptically for several minutes, finally said,
"Be you the fellow what writes the Washington letter for
our paper?" I admitted the charge, and he commented:
"Wal, you don't look like you could write nothing." I felt
that way too.

While the organization was at its height, the Senators
from those three States where the union had a large membership were highly friendly, particularly Senator Morris
Sheppard of Texas, a consistent prohibitionist.

The Klan was very strong in all these States, and a good
many members of this farmer organization had joined it. In
several places they took me to the meetings, usually in
groves, and rather carefully guarded. While going to a meeting in southwest Oklahoma, I stopped off at Colgate, in that
State, where I was scheduled to talk later that week at a
farmer's picnic. As per instructions I went to the office of a
real-estate man who was cooperating with the Union in organizing its cooperative stores. During our conversation a
man drove up and called out the realtor. On coming back,
my friend asked me if I had any idea what the man wanted.
Of course I hadn't, so he informed me that he was a leader
of the Klan and that they wanted to know what my business
was in Colgate and, after finding out, the Klansman told
him I would not be allowed to speak, for the Klan would
drive me out of town, and in the meantime they would open
my mail.

I have never liked the varmints; and so told the realtor to
inform the gentleman that if I could prove he had tampered
with my mail, I would ask the Post Office Department to
prosecute him and that I would be back the morning of

the scheduled picnic and would make my slated address. He advised me to cut out the meeting but though I was not too anxious to make a speech, having made several hundred in my life, I was very anxious not to be prevented from making this one. I showed up on schedule.

It was a glorious day in Colgate, and nearly 2,500 were in the park where I was to speak from a rather shaky wooden platform. All the leaders of the local Farm-Labor Union were there, and most of them begged me to "pass it up." Instead of that I started my talk, really wondering if it were to be my last, by telling the story of this man's visit to the real-estate office. Then I roared at all the Klansmen present: "I don't believe in Government by Wall Street or by White Sheet."

From the applause and cheers that went up, I knew I was safe—for a few minutes. So I proceeded to "pour it on" about conditions in the United States and suggested the program of the Union, which was by that time backing our program of taxation, public ownership, and a Government Marketing Corporation, in addition to cooperative buying and selling for farmers. There were no casualties this time either, but enough dirty looks to convince me that I got off luckily.

In the spring of 1926 Jacob Baker, then director of a liberal publishing house in New York, asked me to write a book on the farm problem. I did so, giving the facts and the prospects for agriculture as I saw them, and as they have come to pass; but after reading it he declined to publish it on the ground that it was too pessimistic, however truthful, and the book would not sell. I then took it to Macmillan, where the manager agreed to have their agricultural expert read it. With hopes, but no expectations, I submitted it; and was not surprised to get the same verdict, that people would not pay for a book that would make them feel badly. We Americans prefer to feel badly without paying for the privilege in cold print.

By 1925 the ardor of many labor leaders for farm-labor cooperation had abated considerably. Some of them told me frankly that they were scared of the competition of bankrupt farmers, and wanted me to urge handouts to them to keep them on the farms. Naturally I remonstrated at making the farmers the goats. Another factor in the de-radicalization of some labor leaders was the fact that they had started labor banks and were out to make dividends for their members. I had it up and down with them on this several times, and once remarked to the presidents of three big labor unions, which had banks, that they were not the same guys I had known before they started these banks.

Among the keenest labor leaders was Warren S. Stone, for many years President of the Brotherhood of Locomotive Engineers, who was absolutely devoted to the interests of his union. When the Engineers bought a coal mine in West Virginia, named after one of their officers, the Prentiss Mine, they objected to unionizing of the miners; and when I asked Stone how come, in his office one day, he was perfectly frank and said with the candor that was one of his characteristics: "It is all wrong. Those miners need a union, but our fellows have put money into this mine and they want dividends. I am in a hell of a spot, but I have got to stand by my own union first." Incidentally, Mr. Stone was vigorously opposed to having the Engineers Bank make its disastrous plunge in real-estate in Sarasota, Florida.

Mr. Stone, like most of the labor leaders I knew in those days and know now, privately realized that general socialization, including ground rent, is essential; but feel their members are not educated up to it. It was, I think, because of his belief in socialization that Warren Stone was personally so anxious to have an independent Labor Party, with a constructive and progressive program for social ownership. He was deeply impressed with the significance of what was being attempted in Russia, and was a financial and moral backer of the cooperative movement, sponsoring one of the first great conventions to develop the cooperative movement among both farmers and labor, held in Chicago in 1921.

Although we had had some success in influencing legislation, the roaring days of the Coolidge Administration took their toll and demonstrated again how difficult it is for principles—and holding of public office—to survive prosperity. By 1927 all the labor unions ended their contributions to the People's Reconstruction League, so we decided to increase our individual membership.

There was a wide hue and cry at the time against monopolies. Following the death of the president of the Reconstruction League, Herbert F. Baker, we re-organized as the Anti-Monopoly League, with George L. Record of New Jersey as president and substantially the same program, with special emphasis upon repealing the special privileges which create monopoly. This lasted about a year, when Mr. Record resigned. Our Board approved asking Professor John Dewey to become President of the organization, and delegated me to extend the invitation to him.

Professor Dewey had been very kind to me, and especially appreciative of the work I had tried to do for children in the Pennsylvania Society to Protect Children from Cruelty. He had not cut me off his list of friends, as several Columbia University professors did, when I opposed America's signing a blank check for Britain in World War I. When I invited him to accept the presidency, he mentioned that he was a philosopher and not a lobbyist. I assured him that I also had never been able to regard any measure, no matter how much I favored it, as a panacea. I was and am unable to see how a dynamic society can have a static economic system, because society will have to be dynamic in order to survive. No "isms" can exterminate that fact.

I told Professor Dewey at this interview also that I had wanted to have the organization called "The People's Lobby," because I felt our program was for the benefit of the entire people, however small the overwhelming demand for it. Professor Dewey said that if we were trying to be a People's Lobby, he would accept the presidency only on the condition that the organization called itself what it tried to be—a "People's Lobby." Our Board accepted his verdict; and thus, so far as I know, the first national "People's Lobby" in America was started.

Professor Dewey cooperated actively and effectvely in the Lobby's work, coming frequently to Washington to meetings, writing and broadcasting for the Lobby, until he withdrew as active President in 1936.

CHAPTER SIX

The Great Depression

In THE SUMMER of 1929 I made my first visit to Europe since 1913, going primarily to attend an international anti-imperialist conference in Frankfort-on-the-Main. I arranged a small conference in Caxton Hall, London, a few days before the Frankfort Conference, on the same subject, at which America's viewpoint could be especially emphasized; and secured the hearty cooperation of the Independent Labor Party in England, of which James Maxton, Member of the House of Commons, was Chairman and Fenner Brockway, Secretary. These two and several other members of that Party attended the Conference, which was fairly well reported in the London papers.

Mr. J. S. Middleton, Secretary of the British Labor Party, wrote in response to my invitation to the Labor Party to participate in the Conference that it could not do so; but did not assign any reason. When I saw him in London a few days before the Conference and asked him the reason, because I knew well the Party's opposition to imperialism, he told me the chief reason was that Roger N. Baldwin, who was a member of our Board at the time and whose name appeared on the letterhead, was a Communist! I assured him that he was mistaken and he was very cordial, as were other members of the Party; and some of them attended the Conference unofficially. Jim Middleton became a warm personal friend, and I always visited with him up to my last European trip in 1939.

The Frankfort Conference was largely organized and at least partly controlled by Communists, for the Communist Party in Russia sensed even then the threat of a "gang-up" against it by all "Christian" capitalist countries. James Maxton was Chairman of the Conference, and he conducted the sessions with dignity, efficiency and fairness. He had a very hard job. A delegate from Europe put him on the spot, but he extricated himself dextrously.

This delegate waved from the platform an American flag which he stated the "rebel" Sandino had captured from American Marines in Nicaragua; and asked a resolution of the Conference expressing the hope that all American Marines invading Nicaragua would be shot, so American control of Nicaragua would be ended. Dr. Harry Laidler and I were among the American delegates, and would have opposed the resolution in that form. Schoolmaster Maxton from Glasgow met the situation with remarkable finesse. He suggested that the proposed expression was hardly appropriate, and as a substitute expressed the hope of the convention that American Marines would be promptly withdrawn from Nicaragua and fighting ended, so that there would be no occasion for the Nicaraguans to fight American soldiers, and that complete independence of Nicaragua would soon be established. The delegates accepted the substitute, which must have been highly gratifying to Mr. Maxton, who was at that time, as at his death in the summer of 1946, an efficient and respected member of the House of Commons.

Believe it or not, at this Conference hardly a word was said against German imperialism, but the imperialisms denounced were chiefly those of the United States, Britain, France, Belgium, and Holland.

In the summer of 1931 Professor Dewey introduced me to Mrs. Ethel Clyde, who at once took the active interest in the Lobby's work, which she continued till it suspended operations in 1950. Hard times had been coming on apace, and though the Lobby's budget was rather small and my own salary about half the earnings of a good plasterer or carpenter, we had a deficit of about $1,500, which Mrs. Clyde paid. Up to that time our monthly *Bulletin* had been stenciled, but now we changed it to an eight-page printed organ for which Mrs. Clyde financed an extensive promotion campaign. Our members were very much pleased with it; and we secured a large number of new subscribers to the *Bulletin*, as well as increasing the membership quite materially, and the *Bulletin* paid its way from then on!

In the early fall of that year, when unemployment and poverty were staggering and the Federal Government was not accepting its responsibility for unemployment, People's Lobby organized a "Joint Committee on Unemployment" in Mrs. Clyde's Park Avenue apartment in New York, to try to arouse, or sting, the Administration into meeting its responsibility. Mrs. Clyde paid all the careful budget of the Committee.

Within a few weeks representatives of the following organizations agreed to cooperate in the Committee's work: Church League for Industrial Democracy; Conference for

Progressive Labor Action; Fellowship of Reconciliation; Labor Bureau, Inc.; People's Lobby; Social Service Commission of the Central Conference of Rabbis; Methodist Federation for Social Service; Workmen's Sick and Death Benefit Association; American Association for Old Age Security; Department of Social Relations, Congregationalist Education Society; Amalgamated Clothing Workers of America; Amalgamated Lithographers of America; New York Teacher's Union; and American Federation of Full-Fashioned Hosiery Workers.

The League for Industrial Democracy offices in New York were the headquarters, and the People's Lobby offices in Washington were the legislative headquarters of the Committee. Professor John Dewey was Chairman of the Committee, and Dr. Sidney E. Goldstein of the Free Synagogue in New York was Chairman of the Executive Committee, with Mary Fox of the League for Industrial Democracy as Secretary-Treasurer. The following were Vice-Chairmen: Harriot Stanton Blatch; Ethel Clyde; John Haynes Holmes; Bishop Francis J. McConnell; Father John A. Ryan; Norman Thomas; and Stephen S. Wise.

Of course the papers gave much publicity, not only because of the merits of the work the Committee was trying to do, but also because representatives of so many organizations were able to work together in peace and amity, for even a noble cause. Newspaper men realize how good and unusual it is for brethren to dwell together in unity.

The Committee had a five point program at its inception:

1. A minimum of $3,000,000,000 for Government construction work to provide jobs for the unemployed.
2. Adequate relief.
3. A 30-hour week law.

4. Liberalized credit terms for the Reconstruction Finance Corporation.

5. Increased estate taxes and income taxes on higher incomes.

Later, taxation of speculative land values and suggestion of the necessity for public ownership was squinted at, but not even all of the organizations represented on the Committee were willing to go as far as this—though most of their representatives were.

The first public event of the Committee was a national conference on the unemployment program for Congress, held in Washington November 30th and December 1st, 1931. This received enormous publicity in the press, and photographers almost outnumbered the large number of reporters covering the Conference. Reports were made on unemployment conditions in the following cities, mainly by representatives who had compiled the information at the Committee's request: Birmingham, Atlanta, Chicago, Minneapolis, Kansas City, St. Louis, New York, Cincinnati, Cleveland, Portland, Philadelphia, Pittsburgh, and Seattle. Addresses at one of the main sessions were broadcast by the National Broadcasting Company.

It is, of course, impossible to determine just what influence this Joint Committee on Unemployment had in securing recognition by the Federal Government of its responsibility for relief and prevention of unemployment; but it was considerable.

The Federal Government has not yet recognized its responsibility to prevent unemployment in the only practical way. It still relies upon deficiteering, or a hot or cold war economy. The Committee did, however, serve a most useful purpose in having representatives appear before Committees of both branches of Congress, urging adequate relief and an interim program to prevent unemployment. It held several conferences in Washington and conducted a nation-wide campaign of publicity and information, till it disbanded in 1935.

During the years it was in operation, I gave a large part of my time to the Committee's work, as representative of the People's Lobby; while Mary Fox put much of her executive ability and experience into the work in the New York office, as representative of the League for Industrial Democracy. Neither of us drew a salary from the Committee.

An illuminating incident early in the Committee's experience was getting the help of Edward F. McGrady, then Legislative Representative of the American Federation of Labor. The Executive Council of the A.F. of L., whom we had asked to cooperate, refused to do so, and instructed Mr. McGrady not to appear at the hearing, early in 1932, on Federal relief, of a Senate Committee, of which Edward P. Costigan from Colorado was Chairman, and Robert M. La Follette, Jr., was ranking Republican. Mr. McGrady appeared however and made a strong statement, and then immediately took part in our nationwide radio broadcast urging such relief. As I knew his Executive Council had opposed it I asked him how he had dared to do it, and he replied, "I told them these poor people need relief and I was going to try to get it for them, and if they didn't like it they could fire me." They didn't!

The Committee sponsored two or three local conferences on unemployment and its program, in St. Louis, New York, and other places, with the work done by volunteers and with very effective publicity.

President Hoover's acquiescence (at least) in the use of the Army to drive the "Bonus Army" out of Washington probably hurt him more than anything else he had done in his term in the White House. I was in New York at the time, and immediately organized a protest meeting in Town Hall, of which Bishop Francis J. McConnell was Chairman, and among the speakers were Dr. Sidney E. Goldstein and Socialist Charles J. Solomon, later a judge in New York City. We had invited various organizations to send representatives and the Hall was fairly well filled. The American Legion and World War Veterans both had representatives and we invited them to speak.

Going into an ante-room during the speeches, I found a middle-aged man sitting in considerable mental distress evidently, and asked him what was the matter, as several other men were giving him dagger looks. He told me that he was gassed in the World War, and had come to speak for the World War Veterans, but that the other gentlemen in the room were from the American Legion and that they wouldn't let him come on to the platform—he had gotten to the meeting late—because they charged him with being a Communist. This they admitted; but I escorted him to the platform and he made a good talk.

Toward 10:30 heckling started in the audience and there were frequent interruptions, so Bishop McConnell adjourned the meeting. The adjournment was formal, but not final; for the audience proceeded to handle the meeting its own way and the several factions indulged in a steady flow of mutual under-valuation, to put it mildly, in loud voices. Someone suggested that we call the police, but when I asked the janitor of the Hall if he wanted that, he thought it would hurt the reputation of the place and also might cost him his job; so we passed that up. He was quick witted, however, and yelled to the leaders of the several factions, "You fellows say you believe in the dictatorship of the proletariat, and I am a proletariat, and have been working here since early this morning." The adversaries saw the point, and left.

In the summer of 1932 representatives of the People's Lobby and the Joint Committee on Unemployment attended the National Conference of Social Work in Philadelphia and presented the program of both organizations at a meeting which we arranged, with anything but the blessing of those in charge of the Conference. Dr. Goldstein made a very strong presentation for the Joint Committee on Unemployment; and as President Hoover had just turned down a plea for Federal aid to children I characterized him in my talk as "The Modern Herod," which caught the headlines.

The meeting was well attended and the publicity was good, but the social workers had not yet sensed en masse that public "relief" was not private charity, but much more important. President Hoover capitulated to the extent of approving a $300,000,000 Federal "loan" for relief. It was never repaid. I had been attending these meetings of social workers off and on for some 30 years, and had never completely gotten over the feeling of being a pariah at them.

In this summer of 1932, also, the People's Lobby helped organize "The Emergency Peace Committee," whose Chairman was Tucker P. Smith of the Fellowship of Reconciliation, and whose Vice-Chairmen were Dorothy Detzer, Secretary of the Women's International League for Peace and Freedom, and Norman Thomas. It included some dozen organizations, and was known as the left wing in the peace movement. A conference held in Washington was well attended and reported. The following were some of the significant statements made at the Conference:

Mr. Chester H. Gray, Washington Representative of the American Farm Bureau Federation, after quoting the reso-

lution of his organization against armaments adopted in
1921 and subsequent resolutions, said:

"So long as great percentages of the annual tax income
of nations—our own included—are devoted to maintaining
military equipment and getting ready for another war, to
say nothing about seeking to pay the obligations incident
to former armed conflicts, just so long may we expect the
people of our nation, and all others, to be borne down below
that status of prosperity which otherwise assuredly could be
experienced.

"Until arms are limited, until nations more actively carry
them into effect by reducing armed equipments, treaties
which academically announce to the world that war is de-
throned, will be somewhat, but not wholly, neutralized so
far as final effect is concerned."

Mr. Fred Brenckman, Washington Representative of the
National Grange, said:

"When we consider that 14 years after the close of the
'war to end wars' finds the world supporting the largest military establishments of history, weighted down with billions
of dollars of debt, and that the nations are now spending
approximately five billion dollars annually for armed defense, it would seem that all sane citizens of every country
would see the imperative necessity of reducing rather than
merely limiting armaments."

William T. Stone, then Washington Representative of
the Foreign Policy Association, said:

"The Disarmament Conference has reached the parting
of the ways. The three great powers which control the des-
tinies of that Conference—the United States, Great Britain
and France—can no longer sidestep the issue which has been
brought to a head by Germany's demand for equality of
rights. France can no longer impose by force unequal provi-

sions of the Versailles Treaty which have been morally repudiated by the enlightened opinion of the world. They must make their choice between a substantial reduction of their own swollen armaments or the repudiation of the Versailles Treaty and the re-armament of Germany."

Dr. J. B. Matthews, then with the Fellowship of Reconciliation, held:

"All efforts at disarmament must confront the vast aggregations of wealth and their political influence represented by the armaments industries of the world. As long as these men are left free to exploit the fears and suspicions of governments and peoples, by pushing the sale of war materials, all the efforts of sentimental peace workers will come to naught."

This was before Dr. Matthews worked for the Dies Committee on Un-American Activities, and turned his back on the principles he had earlier doubtless sincerely espoused.

In 1932 I attended the great Conference against War and Fascism in Amsterdam. This was, like the earlier Frankfort Conference, largely sparked by members or adherents of the Communist Parties in Europe and Asia. It was a most enthusiastic conference with a brilliant speech by Henri Barbusse, showing the growing power and arrogance of international capital.

The winter of 1932–1933 was bleak in temperature and feeling. Hoover's efforts to get President-elect Roosevelt to cooperate with him in helping to solve the most pressing problems were not successful. Governor Roosevelt's brain-trust was still aborning, and Washington was in a state of suspended inanimation. The President's closing of the banks in March 1933, so he could save them and depositors from their own cupidity and stupidity, was hailed by financial interests. Though no one can even now be sure, the verdict of history probably will be that conditions were so shot in America in early March 1933 that the President could have put through any basic economic changes which he wished to, without effective opposition by selfish financial interests. He could easily have taken over the banking and credit system. He did not. He started out to save the profit system, and neither he nor any one else could or can do it.

Professor John Dewey wrote an article for the June issue of our *Bulletin* that year, from which the following is quoted, because it stated so accurately the position of the People's Lobby:

"Superficial treatment of the basic causes which have produced a depression, not only in the United States but throughout the world, will not end the depression. It may help some of the victims—but at best only temporarily.

"Emergency measures imply that they are directed to meet an emergency, but the present world-wide chaos is not a condition from which the world can emerge on a basis of assured and general prosperity, without fundamental changes in the economic systems of every major nation, except Russia.

"America's problems cannot be settled on a narrow nationalistic basis. Every major economic issue of every nation is international, and cannot be settled upon a strictly legalistic basis, nor upon standards of international ethics which have hitherto passed muster.

"Practical international cooperation must be substituted for international rivalry. This means adjustment of international debts, of loans from capital export to capital import countries, of titles to natural resources, and of concessions held by foreigners, as well as adjustment of tariffs and other barriers to freedom of exchange.

"Obviously our immediate problem in America is to secure a redistribution of the national income not merely in numbers of dollars but in actual purchasing power. We cannot do this merely by taxing incomes, estates and corporation surpluses, essential as these are. Debts and interest rates must be written down and utility charges reduced.

"It is still true that so long as cities and states tax buildings and other labor products, instead of obtaining the major part of their income from the taxation of land values, the land owner will be the residual beneficiary of expenditures by the Federal Government for relief and for made work, as well as the beneficiary of public improvements and other ordinary municipal and state expenditures, which increase the selling price of land."

All these facts, with figures, had been given President-elect Roosevelt.

In April that year, an economist working with the Government, on the "New Deal," asked me if I had any money to invest. I thanked him but assured him I had not, and asked him why he inquired. He told me he was helping draft the National Industrial Recovery Act, and that it was going to produce the greatest "bull" stock market America had ever had. I expressed my surprise that the President would lend himself to this, and said I thought the New Deal claimed to be devoted to labor and consumers. My New Deal economist friend told me to be myself, and assured me there was going to be a killing in the stock market while the effects of the new economic salvation were operating.

People have asked me why I was not a "New Dealer." This incident and plenty of similar ones, including the record before and since the starting of the new Paradise in Washing, reveal the reasons.

In May of that year the National Industrial Recovery Act was introduced in both branches of Congress, and I appeared to suggest amendments which I hoped would prevent the results which my New Deal economist friend had forecast for it. I was given a scant five minutes before the House Committee on Ways and Means, to which it was referred because it carried a tax provision to raise the revenue for public works amortization. At that session the bill was endorsed by the President of the U.S. Chamber of Commerce and by William Green, President of the A.F. of L., in equally glowing terms, while Mr. Green said that, if necessary, he would endorse a sales tax to pay for the public works.

We went down the elevator together, and he said to me: "Ben, didn't I make a good speech?" I couldn't resist the chance, and told him I thought it about the bummest speech I had heard any labor leader make in a long time and that if he didn't know no sales tax was necessary to finance recovery he didn't know enough to be President of the A.F. of L.

The Senate Committee on Finance gave me three quarters of an hour to analyze the bill with the joint introducer, Senator Robert F. Wagner of New York, present. I told the Committee that it was a gigantic swindle, whatever the introducers meant it to be, which would validate scores of billions of watered stock and meant a stock market boom but wouldn't settle a single problem, nor help labor or consumers, but just the reverse, in the long run. This much of my statement was excised, though I invited Senator Wagner to show where I was wrong.

Following are excerpts from my statement at the Senate Committee hearings:

"The preamble to the industrial recovery bill stating the purpose is to remove obstructions to the free flow of interstate commerce, which tend to diminish the amount thereof, is misleading. Production and commerce are limited by the inequitable distribution of the national income, with one fiftieth of the families getting nearly one fifth of the national income, by high land values, which constitute a brake of 6 or 7 billion dollars a year on prosperity, and by about $160,000,000,000 of (long term) debt, with its annual tribute of at least $7,000,000,000 a year, by patent laws, by private banking and by taxes on consumption.

"The House bill increases obstructions on commerce by increasing sales taxes, and the Wagner bill would be little help, unless amended to give the Federal Government complete control over capitalization, profits and prices in industry, and over retail prices and rents, as well as making the shorter work week and the minimum wage mandatory.

"I do not debate this bill, Mr. Chairman, on the grounds of legality. I know that when strict constitutional observance has led the Nation to the point where 4 percent of the people own about four fifths of the wealth, the thing is so serious that I very much doubt whether the Supreme Court of the United States—I know it has no legal right to—would assume to declare unconstitutional any legislation which Congress decides to be necessary to meet this situation."

I also submitted to the Committee, and had incorporated in the record, a brief on paying for recovery as we go, or doing most of it, prepared as an amendment to the Revenue Act of 1932, by Joseph J. Wexler, Certified Public Accountant and tax expert of New York. The Committee declined to call either Mr. Wexler or Professor Joseph J. McGoldrick of Columbia University, a tax expert, later Comptroller of the City of New York.

The People's Lobby appeared that year at many Committee hearings on New Deal measures.

CHAPTER SEVEN

War Prevents a Bigger Depression

IN 1934 I went to Russia with a party which included Ethel Clyde, Margaret Sanger, Professor E. A. Ross of Wisconsin and Professors Raymond Walsh and Robert Lamb, then of Harvard University. Professor Ross, who had spent months in Russia shortly after the Revolution and traveled from Vladivostock to Leningrad, was keenly impressed with the progress, but not completely assured that democratic processes could be fully maintained as long as Russia was subject to attack from several sides.

In Leningrad our party met up with a party Sherwood Eddy was conducting, as he did for years, and through his courtesy we heard a talk by Carl Radek in Moscow. Soon after we got there Margaret Sanger was invited to attend a luncheon at which the Commissar of Health discussed the Government's program for the Nation's health. Through an interpreter she asked him what Russia's Five Year Plan for population was and he replied: "To increase it as rapidly as possible; we hope to have 200,000,000 people by the end of this decade."

Mrs. Sanger returned to the hotel thoroughly disgusted, and declared she would carry her campaign to India, China and Japan. She didn't have much more luck—though more cooperation—in those nations. The Russians remembered the many times their country had been invaded since 1917, and may have anticipated Hitler's invasion within a few short years.

One of the most illuminating speeches were two talks which the Professors of our party and I had with a Russian who had lived in the United States for several years, working in Detroit most of the time, and had gone back after the Revolution. He told a story about Stalin, probably not true, but showing some freedom of criticism—then. While Stalin was driving to Georgia for a rest, he stopped on the road to talk to a peasant, who was leading a heavily laden donkey. About noon the donkey got hungry and started to bray, and the peasant said, "Well, Comrade Stalin, my donkey is hungry, and I have got to feed him." "Huh," Stalin said, "in Russia there are 160 million donkeys braying, but I don't pay the slightest attention to them."

I rode from Moscow, the only city in Russia besides Leningrad I visited that trip, to Warsaw with Brewer Eddy. On the way we got to discussing American supporters of foreign missions and compared notes on the experiences I had had raising money for the Congregationalist Foreign Mission Board and Mr. Eddy's current efforts for this Board. He told me that in a few weeks he was to meet his brother Sherwood in China, and they would have a two months campaign there against Communism! I asked him if Sherwood and he would run a two months campaign against the crimes of Christian capitalism when they got back to the United States and he replied, "Of course not, I am raising money for foreign missions."

Naturally on my return to America I was quizzed as to what I thought of Russia. I admitted no one should pass judgement on a nation till he had lived in it for a long time and knew its history, peoples and problems; but I thought Americans should be equally grateful to Russia for two things—showing us some things that we need to do, and equally showing us how not to try to do those things.

Soon after World War Two, when I was testifying before the House Committee on Ways and Means on a tax bill, the Republican whip in the House, Harold Knutson of Minnesota, remarked he had heard I had been in Russia and he wanted to know what I thought of the Russian system. Every member of the Committee listened most carefully, and the Chairman Robert L. Doughton of North Carolina cupped his "lame" ear and leaned forward to catch my answer, being taken down in shorthand. I explained the impression I had gotten on my first trip, confirmed by my second, and said I hadn't changed. Mr. Doughton commented "fair enough," and no one called me "subversive."

I am equally convinced that Russia and every nation in which, as Prof. John Dewey stated about Russia after visiting the country, "the Government is trying to educate its people for a cooperative instead of a competitive economy," is entitled to at least fifty years free from threat of invasion before judgement is passed on its economic system. Russia has not had five consecutive years of such freedom since the 1917 Revolution!

On that trip I spent a few days in Berlin checking up on what the Nazis were actually doing, and had an opportunity to discuss matters with national and city officials, through letters of introduction from the Counsellor of the German

Embassy in Washington and from our Ambassador, Dr. William E. Dodd.

As usual I spent a good deal of time with the British Labor Party in London, and introduced Professors Walsh and Lamb to Jim Middleton, Secretary of the British Labor Party, who very kindly helped us meet key people in Britain.

In the summer of 1935 Mrs. Clyde, Dr. John H. Gray, our Treasurer, former President of the American Economic Association, and I made a follow-up trip to Russia, which Dr. Gray had last visited in 1931. In Vienna at the Friends Service House we saw some of the victims of the local Nazi brutality, including men who had recently gotten out of jail; but an Austrian labor leader, who had been for some time in the United States, told us significantly that Austria had no future as Austria. It would have to be combined with some other country.

In my appearance before the Senate Committee holding hearings on the President's "Court Packing" plan, I suggested it should be postponed till Congress enacted some intelligent legislation, to see what the court would do. Senator Burke, Chairman, turned livid; but recovered in time to thank me for my testimony.

Dr. Colston E. Warne of Amherst College was elected President of the Lobby in 1936 to succeed Dr. Dewey, who was resigning from active work in most organizations.

In my trip to Europe that year I had several conferences with Mr. Francis Williams, then the financial editor and later the managing editor of the London *Daily Herald*, unofficial organ of the British Labor Party. He knew Germany was arming, and tried to wake his country to the need for a different economic program to meet Germany's requirements and to prevent an explosion in Europe. In a striking series of articles in his paper, he urged international organization along the following lines:

"If the people of the world want peace, they must be prepared to plan for it. Only by a peace plan, realistic and precise, can we hope to reverse international policies that are leading directly to war. . . .

"The proposal to call an international Conference to consider the problems of political insecurity and economic inequality among nations can be made a turning point of history, if this time we are really prepared to plan constructively for peace. . . .

"If this conference fails we may well see an end for a generation to all hope of world peace by negotiation. . . .

"Increasingly modern war becomes a matter of control of resources of essential raw materials and foodstuffs.

"British Imperialism has sufficient charges, well founded and serious to meet, without accepting responsibility for the political and economical crimes committed against German people by their present rulers."

He was backed in this by the British Labor Party, but did not succeed.

That fall Norman Thomas told me that in a recent talk President Roosevelt told him he knew he should be backing the loyalists in Spain, but was going along with our "nonintervention" in the Civil War, which meant backing Hitler and Mussolini, because he needed the Catholic vote. I think he misjudged the progressivism of rank and file American Catholics, though the hierarchy was putting on a tremendous campaign for reaction.

Early in 1936 Mr. Irving Brant, biographer of Madison, author of "Storm Over The Constitution" and other books, and at the time chief editorial writer for the St. Louis *Star-Times,* wrote a short pamphlet for the Lobby called "Government Monopolies Are Constitutional," which Senator Lynn Frazier of North Dakota read into the *Congressional Record* for us so that it could be more widely circulated. The following brief quotations show why the Dixiecrats in 1948, and the Dixiecrat-Standpat-Republican Congressional coalition since then, didn't use this pamphlet as a textbook for their campaigns.

"Madison wrote: 'Let the national government be armed with a positive and complete authority in all cases where uniform measures are necessary. As in trade etc., etc. Let it also retain the powers which it now possesses. Let it have a negative in all cases whatsoever on the legislative acts of the states as the King of Great Britain heretofore had. This I conceive to be essential and the least possible abridgement of the state sovereignties.'

"Alexander Hamilton said in the Constitutional Convention that states as states 'ought to be abolished.' Madison asked for a government 'which would most approximate the states to the condition of countries.' Gouverneur Morris said of the states: 'We cannot annihilate, but we may take the teeth out of the serpents.'

"All we need is to go back to the Founding Fathers and learn from them what federal power means. The power is the Constitution."

His pamphlet was an unanswerable reply to the claims the American Liberty League was making that the United States Government has no power to control agriculture or industry along the lines attempted by the Roosevelt administration. Sensing this was a good topic for a radio debate I asked Mr. Brant to take the affirmative, and tried to get a conservative to claim "Government Monopolies are not Constitutional." John W. Davis, Wall Street lawyer and Democratic Candidate for President in 1924, declined. James A.

Emery, Counsel for the National Association of Manufacturers, said: "Of course they are constitutional, but they are d - - - - foolish." I assured him few people were less qualified than he to pass on their wisdom. I besought the U.S. Chamber of Commerce, Liberty League and other commercial bodies to provide a negative speaker but with no success. Mr. Brant had to talk, not debate.

Of course the constitutionality of government regional monopolies or even national ones doesn't mean they are wise, unless operated as part of an over-all Government plan. Topsy, who just grew, is not a model for an efficient democracy.

When Dr. Warne resigned for his sabbatical half year of travel in 1937, Bishop Francis J. McConnell was elected President of the People's Lobby, a position he held several years, giving most valuable help in the Lobby's work.

Early in 1937 it was evident that the efforts of the "New Deal" to save a water-logged economy were failing. Leon Henderson gave repeated warnings that the economy was slipping, and was backed by more conservative economists. A shot in the arm was needed and preparations for a war could be a substitute for basic economic changes and ending special privileges—to which the Democratic Party too often gives lip service, instead of action service.

President Roosevelt, having helped the aggressors Hitler and Mussolini via Franco in Spain, burst forth with his Chicago "quarantine the aggressor" speech, which was widely acclaimed by profit-hungry industrial and financial interests, which were shrewd enough to know Roosevelt's unlimited capacity to fool a lot of people a good deal of the time.

America started sending war material to Britain and Japan!

At one of the Lobby's luncheon broadcasts that spring Leon Henderson upset the complacency of labor leaders by stating wages can never keep up with prices—of course under a chaotic economy such as ours.

After three years of the New Deal, Eleanor Roosevelt admitted it had only been "buying time" and had not made any of the needed economic changes. Her husband didn't intend to; he was the slickest and by no means most scrupulous economic royalist America had produced since Alexander Hamilton, father of the protective tariff and private fortunes.

In 1938 and 1939 I made my summer vacation trips to Europe; also speaking trips to the Pacific Coast, as in many years.

From Britain's declaration of war on Germany in September 1939 on, it was quite obvious that every effort would be made by the President and the financial and other interests to get America into the Second World War. The financial interests and the President both wanted to save the profit system. They differed as to domestic policies to do this, but were in full agreement that our participation in a big war, whether as "arsenal" or as "arsenal-and-expeditionary-force," would give the system of "private enterprise" a short lease of life.

Certain impressions I gathered on my four trips to Europe from 1935 to 1939 bear directly upon World War Two. Our party was in Geneva while the Ethiopian campaign was at its hottest and heard Sir Samuel Hoare make his speech to the Assembly of the League, in which he discussed the possibility of an international conference to consider the distribution of raw materials. It was a gesture, and nothing came of it except a slight appeasement of people who objected to having four great nations, including our own, hold such a large proportion of the world's natural resources.

The tenseness in Europe which increased steadily since 1936 was so apparent even here, in the summer of 1938, that I debated whether I should make the trip to Europe that year. Discretion lost, and I decided to spend most of my time in Geneva, after my usual visit with the British Labor Party leaders. There I tried to get the sentiment of the people in the Secretariat of the League, and in the International Labor Organization, on the prospects in Europe.

The opinion of the majority of these well informed experts was about as follows:

"1. The fractionizing of Europe on racial, instead of organization on economic lines, by the Treaty of Versailles and subsequent treaties, was a serious mistake.

"2. Substantial revisions of present geographic boundaries can be made by adjustments, without armed conflict, within the next three to five years, leading to the moderate Federation of Europe within a decade or so, when the League of Nations would be able to function and not merely to exist.

"3. The real conflict of the next decade in Europe will be not between nations but between economic systems.

"4. In a war between Germany, and Britain and France, the Baltic League, Poland and most Danubian states would be neutral or with Germany."

A year showed that they were too optimistic as to revisions of boundaries by adjustment, correct on point three, and way off on point four.

Through our American Embassy, I secured an interview in the summer of 1938 with the French *Chef de Cabinet* in the Ministry of Colonies, of which Georges Mandel was Minister, in Paris, and discussed with him the British Labor Party's plan for international controls and for ending the

system of national mandates. I asked him point blank
whether any private organization or any Government department in France favored this plan, with which, he had
assured me, he was familiar. He said there was no such
sentiment; and when I asked whether he did not feel that
the alternative to this was a war, he replied, "Unquestion-
ably, but France intends to keep her Empire." The size of
that Empire was well known, and the methods by which
it was acquired.

Late in the summer of 1939 I started on my visit to four
vital capitals—London, Copenhagen, Stockholm, and Paris.
In London I had several long conferences with members of
the House of Commons, including Hugh Dalton, F. V.
Alexander, a leader in the cooperative movement, and James
Maxton. Mr. Dalton was anxious to have me do all possible
to get Americans to realize the seriousness of the situation,
and to back Britain to the limit.

I told him that in my judgment it would be difficult to
get the progressives, and probably the liberals in America,
much as they despised Hitler's methods, to underwrite
Britain's conflict, unless there was assurance that after the
war the British Labor Party would have more influence in
the peace terms and post-war world organization than following World War One, and I asked him if there were any
such assurance. He was frank to admit that he could not
give it, and I usually found frankness among other leaders
of the British Labor Party on this subject. Mr. Dalton felt
then that a new order would result from the war, but questioned how far Britain would go towards socializing during
a war. It took the 1945 election to change the post-war prospects.

As I was saying goodbye to Jim Middleton, early in August 1939, I raised the same point with him, and his response

was: "Don't forget the inevitability of gradualness." I commented on the fact that I had heard that injunction for at least two decades, and asked him if he didn't realize that Britain would probably be at war within six weeks largely due to the profit system. He admitted it.

British labor had had the opportunity to get essential changes peacefully twice, in the first and second governments.

In Copenhagen a member of the Cabinet, to whom I was introduced by a labor leader, asked me whether I would advise Denmark to resist Hitler if he invaded the country. I asked whether this would be in the expectation Britain would come to their help, and he said, "Yes."

"With what?" I asked.

Sorrowfully, he responded: "You have answered my question."

In Stockholm a member of the Swedish Cabinet put practically the same question to me, and of course I gave him the same answer. To my question whether Sweden's prosperity was due chiefly to their public ownership and cooperative movement or to the fact Sweden had been re-arming Germany for some years, this official replied promptly: "To the fact we have been re-arming Germany."

In Paris the gayness had vanished; determination was evident. I got back five days before Hitler marched into Poland.

After his election as President of the Lobby in 1936, Dr. Colston E. Warne wrote in our June *Bulletin*:

"Franklin Delano Roosevelt has for three years been in the unhappy position of seeking to balance an unstable economic structure. He has tried scores of measures. He has undoubtedly been sincere—and persevering. Today he is being condemned by the very business groups whose interests he has been attempting to preserve. Regimentation, bureaucracy, spendthrift, boondoggler, autocrat, bolshevik are words hurled at his administration by Liberty Leaguers and other flag wavers.

"I do not undertake to defend Mr. Roosevelt. I think that he has been trying to do the impossible. I do want to make the record clear as to what he has been doing. In three years he has bulwarked the private debt structure by loans, subsidies, and purchases of preferred stock. He has introduced inflationary devices to pull the debtors out of the red. He has forced extensive reserves into the banks by bond sales to the Federal Reserve System. He has made a large section of business highly profitable by his price policies. He has, hopefully, made the business world freer from wild-cat stock schemes and the rigging of the market. He has, despite opposition, sought to simplify the financial structure. He has pumped funds into circulation through relief grants and public works expenditures, saving the business world from the immediate worry of civil uprising. He has advanced military expenditures to unprecedented heights— always a boon to business.

"To buy out the present owners of industry at the present valuations that they place upon their holdings would be folly. Five years of drastic taxation of income, of corporate surplus, of land values, of undivided profits and of estates, would lower their estimation of the worth of their holdings.

"It would be a bold prophet who would predict with confidence that the present owners of our country would submit to socialization without resorting to violence in defiance of the democracy which they pretend to uphold. That problem lies ahead. But the need of today is to press the need of taxation as a prelude to socialization of our industries."

Oscar Ameringer correctly stated that the business and special privilege interests which were so bitterly assailing President Roosevelt were "sassing their savior." Their stupidity was the President's greatest asset with the masses. The pump was primed; but chiefly for owners, not for consumers.

CHAPTER EIGHT

Luring Americans into the War

THE SLOW and tragic steps by which America refused to take measures to prevent war, and on the contrary fomented war, under the President's direction, constitute a terrific indictment of uninformed democracy. In the September 1936 *Bulletin* of the People's Lobby, I wrote an article based upon my trip to Europe that summer, entitled "Britain and France Veer Right to Fascism and War," in which I quoted a statement by Franz Neumann:

"Monopoly-economy . . . which is based on monopoly rents, must collapse in a negative state as soon as a really grave economic crisis occurs. . . .

"Therefore, monopoly capital overthrows democracy and establishes the dictatorship of a so-called totalitarian-interventionist state, which guarantees monopoly rents, gags the workers, and enslaves the citizens. The German cartel system, brought to the verge of financial ruin by the economic crisis of 1930–32, has been saved by the fascist state."

I analyzed the results of the "Front Populaire" in France, and the record of the British Labor Party, in and out of office. I also quoted in this article an editorial "Divide and Conquer" from *The New Statesman and Nation* (London) of August 15 that year, on the Spanish situation, severely taking the British Government to task and saying:

"And so by our invariable retreats we make the danger that we dread. Fascism, now an international coalition, has grown by our hesitation incomparably more formidable than it was in its origins. Trading on our timidity and our disunion, it has evolved a swift and daring technique of action to which we oppose no common strategy of defense. Immune from effective resistance it will at last provoke one of us, in sheer self-preservation, to a war that unity and courage might have prevented."

Some of our members thought my conclusions very pessimistic and unrealistic.

In every way possible the People's Lobby backed the plan suggested by Francis Williams, then Financial Editor of the *London Daily Herald,* for calling an international economic conference to offset the failure of the World Economic Conference in London in the summer of 1933.

The Board of Directors of the People's Lobby considered our international economic program repeatedly and carefully. There was agreement that before America should give assurance of money, men, munitions or even moral support to a war, except for defense, there must be assurance that the governments of nations we back would accept the following program:

"1. Financing of war preparedness by current taxation.

"2. Nationalization of banking and credit, of the munitions industry and of natural resources.

"3. A referendum on war similar to that provided by the LaFollette Resolution.

"4. Placing all colonies under an International Mandates System Control.

"5. International control of:

    (a) Natural resources.

    (b) Ocean borne commerce.

"6. Relative freedom of exchange.

"7. European nations and Britain to agree to gradual organization of Europe on an economic basis, instead of on the present racial or nationalistic basis."

In November 1938 I stated in a public address at Springfield College (Mass): "The President's frantic appeal for a big re-armament program, while avowedly designed to establish protectorate over Latin-America, which the Latin-Americans apparently don't want, is really to get the Democratic party and its office holders out of the jam they face in 1940. . . .

"The President needs a Franco victory in Spain to justify his rearmament program, for while the expulsion of the rebel Franco would not ensure peace and prosperity in Spain, it would put a crimp in the Berlin-Rome axis for quite a spell, and the President couldn't use those bogeys over South America as a reason for his naval splurge.

"The President knew why he wanted the embargo on arms to Spain, and knows why he doesn't want it removed.

"He views 1940 with trepidation."

Each year, 1936 to 1939, I made my trips to Europe, and afterwards my speaking trips to the Pacific Coast, pointing out in practically all of my talks that America was heading toward a war, without action by the people. In discussing the Neutrality Act, early in 1939, before the House Committee on Foreign Affairs, I stated that "America would not be safe with a President who takes orders from the Vatican and British imperialists, even when they coincide, as on Spain."

On September 21, 1939, the Board of Directors of the People's Lobby adopted a statement on the war, reading in part:

"Before America allies herself with any nations, through changing our neutrality laws so that under existing conditions munitions, airplanes and the products of our farms, factories, mines and oil fields, or our credit, become available to any belligerent nation, the following minimum program of national legislation should be enacted."

It then outlined our program for drastic taxation and for socialization of natural resources, natural monopolies, and basic industries, with substantially the British Labor Party's program of international controls, and concluded:

"In addition, Congress should stipulate that the British and French Governments should state their war aims, and make public now any secret treaties they have in force, and the terms of their agreements with Turkey and other nations with regard to their attitude in the present conflict.

"Americans have a right to all facts bearing on our possible participation, by any means, in World War II. They did not have them with respect to World War I—with disastrous consequences, which we do not wish to see repeated under the indefinite plea to crush even such an abomination as Hitlerism."

The Lobby was severely criticized by some factions, but there was little reduction in our publicity and probably in the influence of the Lobby.

In 1939 Senator Frazier read into the *Congressional Record* an article which I wrote in our *Bulletin*, "Americans Must Win War on Poverty or Be Kidded into Foreign Wars."

We had over 100,000 of the reprints of this widely distributed throughout the country.

The contrast between Washington's treatment of those opposed to America's entrance into the war in 1917 and in 1941 was very striking. Earlier I have given some of the incidents of the hectic times and treatment accorded honest protestants on World War I. In 1941, both before and after Germany attacked Russia, the sentiment was very different. On World War II there was general feeling that as America hadn't prevented war she must defend herself, and probably defend the Western Hemisphere. There was wide disapproval of the waste and inefficiency in the defense program, and in the control thereof by selfish and profiteering interests.

An investigation which the People's Lobby had made early in 1941 of dollar-a-year men and volunteers in the defense program from war industries receiving enormous defense contracts, got wide publicity in the farm and labor press, and the article summarizing it was read into the *Congressional Record* by Representative John M. Coffee, in August 1941, as he had earlier read into the *Record* a radio speech by Bishop Francis J. McConnell, as President of the People's Lobby, broadcast at one of our luncheons, "What Peace Terms Do We Want?"

In 1917 we had had four years of the "New Freedom," and conditions were pretty bad and threatening to become worse, although America's supplying of the Allies had helped the economic situation somewhat. In 1941 there had been eight years of the New Deal, and only a small sale of American products, farm and manufactured, to France till her fall, and to Britain.

The lesson of the earlier war had not been lost, however. There were few well organized and effective institutions working against America's participation in World War I. In 1941 there were several "peace" organizations, the National Council for the Prevention of War, the Carnegie Peace Foundation, the America First Committee, Keep America Out of War Congress, the Youth Committee Against War, and the highly alert Women's International League for Peace and Freedom; but only a few of them fully realized or admitted the economic causes of war.

There had been in the meantime the investigation of the munitions industry by the Senate Committee of which Gerald P. Nye was Chairman.

The Catholic church, heavily responsible for Hitler's growth and power through backing his man Friday—Franco —in Spain, had hated bitterly to see Hitler allied with Russia, but hated even more the prospect that Hitler might be defeated by Russia.

New factors and influences appeared in the picture in 1940 and 1941; for the financial interests, which openly took the lead in World War I for American intervention with expeditionary forces, worked more in 1940 and 1941 through agencies such as "The Committee to Defend America by Aiding the Allies."

An illustration of the changed attitude was the resolution adopted at the Keep America Out of War Congress in the Nation's capital over Labor Day week end in 1941, at which by a vote of about two to one, the delegates from all over the United States advocated public ownership of defense and other basic industries as essential to real defense and to make peace terms and post-war organizations practical and just. This marked a distinct advance, in thought, not in achievement.

By late 1941 our involvement in the World War was obviously inevitable. Nathaniel Peffer stated in the *New Re-*

public, December 22, 1941, after Pearl Harbor: "In the end the tensions have always resolved themselves into a confrontation of the United States and Japan, whatever nations were in dispute in the first instance." Regarding our attitude to Japan, Mr. Peffer stated: "Partly, probably mostly, it lies in the economic stake which the development of China offers, and the unwillingness of the United States to permit any other power to appropriate that stake."

As far back as 1937 a long-time friend of President Roosevelt had warned me that the President had had a life-long ambition to be a war-time President—not that he liked slaughter, but that he envisioned himself as a world leader and able to bring order out of world chaos, through war—the fatal messianic complex. The President, of course, was fortunate in that God had provided him with a people too largely economic illiterates, and with a perfect radio voice; but there couldn't be a worse indictment of a people than to fall for a Roosevelt.

I had talked with State Senator Franklin D. Roosevelt at Albany, but never saw him as President, as I never saw President Coolidge or President Hoover in the White House, where I talked more than once with Wilson and Harding.

My experiences in World War I, noted earlier, made me wonder what my fate was to be in World War II; for I had continuously pointed out that the "New Deal" policies were making war inevitable because they made international cooperation impossible.

The Board of Directors of the Lobby at their January 1941 meeting adopted a resolution asking that the life of the Lend-Lease bill be limited to one year, and that Congress in joint session elect one United States Senator and one member of the House of Representatives, a Republican and a Democrat, to advise with the President on every power granted him under the proposed bill—the President to act only if one of the two members approved, otherwise Congressional action to be required—all based on the President's assurance he would not send an American army overseas, except for actual defense.

All through 1941, up to Pearl Harbor, I worked unofficially with organizations opposed to America's entrance into the war without at least some assurance that it wouldn't be just World War I over again; and reported the situation pretty fully in the People's Lobby *Bulletin*.

Bishop Francis J. McConnell, President of the People's Lobby, at one of our luncheons in March 1941, broadcast by the National Broadcasting Company, said:

"What is to be the peace aim of the leaders of Britain, or the British Government? The question is, after this war is over, what is the aim of the British people, and aside from the mere matter of self-defense of the Empire or of the Nation, on what grounds are they asking for aid from the American people?"

We printed in our *Bulletin* early that year, a statement by Raymond Clapper, ace columnist of the Scripps-Howard newspapers:

"This war rose as much out of an unfair distribution of raw-material resources as out of any one thing, although there were other contributing causes.

"A considerable proportion of these raw materials is under British and Dutch control. The Japanese have wanted to get at those materials in the East Indies. Germany and Italy have wanted to get at those which lie in Africa."

Late in 1940, it seemed to me that Germany would soon end the pact with Russia which Hitler had made so he wouldn't have a real war on two fronts and which Russia accepted to get more time to defend herself from Germany. I went to Eugene Meyer, then owner of the *Washington Post,* to ask if he wouldn't use his influential paper to try to get Russia to break away and join the western nations at once. In his office he looked at me quizzically and asked, "What do you think this war is being fought for?" I told him I had my own suspicions, but would like to know his views. He replied: "So that when the Triple Axis is knocked out, Britain and we can run the world, and we don't need any help from Russia. Besides the Russians can neither fight nor produce."

He then called in his secretary and chief editor, and with maps, a globe and diagrams pointed out where British and American possessions, investments and trade were, to explain the belief of many Americans and Britishers that the two countries didn't need Russian help to substitute Anglo-American world domination for the Axis attempt to dominate.

Henry Luce's dream of the "American Century" had a much wider vogue than Henry Wallace's "Century of the Common Man," but the "American Century" and the "Russian Century" couldn't co-exist. The "Century of the Common Man"—regardless of color and previous condition of servitude—doesn't want either one. The *Post,* however, has been one of the fairest of America's newspapers in supporting human rights and genuine internationalism.

CHAPTER NINE

World War II

FROM THE DECLARATION of war, right after Pearl Harbor, People's Lobby urged two things repeatedly, before committees of Congress and in broadcasts, news stories and talks over the nation:

1. That the Government should take over all plants essential for war production and should direct agricultural production, making processors and distributors of farm products agencies of the Government, with equipment pooled and profits restricted, as in Britain.

2. That the Government pay for the war through taxes based on ability to pay and benefits received from Government, or as we put it tersely, "pay-as-you-go through pay-as-you-can."

This program was not adopted by Congress, as it would have cooled patriotism to the freezing point. It was not even approved by any major farm or labor organization, and as employment in war industries increased it was tragically evi-

125

dent that the main objective of all industry, of landed farmers and of too much of organized labor was to get as much
out of the war trough as possible—and to let some one else
fill the trough.

I told the Senate Finance Committee when appearing on
one of the war revenue bills, that about the only thing
Americans were unanimously behind in the war was letting
the other fellow pay for it.

The attitude of most members of committees of Congress
before which I appeared on various measures was in striking
contrast to the treatment I sometimes got during World
War I at such hearings. In quite blunt language I discussed
the folly of this war, and its preventability, particularly before Senate committees, charging that conditions were so
bad here we just had to have a war to cover up on the break-
down, and that apparently our idea of preventing war was
first to arm countries and provide them with material to
fight us, and cajole them into war, instead of making some
plan to prevent war.

I quoted the statement of Leon Henderson that it was
very unfair to say the Japanese were selfish, because they
had shot back at us all the munitions and equipment we had
sold them. No vocal exception was taken by any committee
member to my statements, though if glares could kill I would
have been dead long ago.

With equal candor I noted to Committees of Congress
that this was the first war in which we had changed sides
since it started in Spain, when the President, under Catholic
pressure, supported Franco by opposing the loyalists and refusing to let munitions and supplies be sent them, thus
building up Hitler and Mussolini and making them what
they were in 1939.

It was years later—March 5, 1946—that Winston Churchill

said in his speech at Westminster College, Fulton, Missouri:

"Up till the year 1933, or even 1935, Germany might have been saved from the awful fate which has overtaken her, and we might all have been spared the miseries Hitler let loose upon mankind.

"There never was a war in all history easier to prevent by timely action than the one which has just desolated such great areas of the globe. It could have been prevented without the firing of a single shot, and Germany might be powerful, prosperous and honored today, but no one would listen, and one by one we were all sucked into the awful whirlpool."

In 1937 while attending the Summer School of the Independent Labor Party in Great Britain, near Letchworth, I noticed an old man crying at the Saturday night dance and asked him:

"What are you crying about, when the young folks are having a really good time?"

He replied: "I'm thinking about the terrible price they will soon have to pay for Britain's three centuries of imperialism."

Churchill's speech was of course designd to get Uncle Sam to share John Bull's role of world stabilizer. President Truman pronounced the benediction on this English-speaking Union concept by his presence at Churchill's speech, in which Britain's War Prime Minister just repudiated by the British people as Peace Prime Minister, gave this ultimatum:

"Neither the sure prevention of war, nor the continuous rise of world organization, will be gained without what I have called the fraternal organization of the English-speaking peoples. This means a special relationship between the British Commonwealth and Empire, and the United States."

Progressives in Congress and in the Administration have

been able to beat down the efforts of reactionaries to cut off economic help to Britain till she ended her socialization program, but Aneurin Bevan has rightly appraised the significance of Churchill's Fulton speech, and President Truman's acquiescence.

A Republican Senator remarked to me in the summer of 1945: "Congress will take from you what it won't from anyone else." He did not add "and like it." Congress knew I was telling the truth, however painful.

A factor which helped me in my many appearances before Committees was a story which the Associated Press sent throughout the country about me as champion of the people, which had a circulation of at least a million, while such magazines as *Pathfinder, Life* and a few more carried squibs; and we got a circulation, many years, of millions on stories which the Lobby put out.

Another factor in my immunity from punishment for untoward veracity was the fact that various committees, such as the Truman, Kilgore and Murray Senate Committees, and the House Tolan Committee, as well as both Senate and House Military and Naval Affairs Committees, were making investigations of the conduct of the war and giving wide publicity to them, so that the moral sensibilities of the American people were somewhat shocked by the condition, so well stated by the late William Allen White (for many years a member of the Lobby) that the business interests which were running the war program were primarily interested in a victory for their stockholders. The capitalist press gave us more space than farm, labor or church papers.

In June 1943, I analyzed the distribution of national income after ten years of the "New Deal" program for the common man, pointing out that it "was a killing *for*—not *of*—economic royalists." The figures given by the Department of Commerce *Survey of Current Business,* showed that while the national income increased from 1932 to 1942 by approximately 200%, wages and salaries in private industry increased only 156%, and income from ownership or control of property increased 661%, or *four times the increase in income from wages and salaries in private industry.* This statement got very wide publicity throughout the nation, though of course, conditions changed later, when labor commenced to get its wartime wage rates, time and a half and double time for overtime.

Labor, agriculture and industry all increased their savings, as the Government increased its debts. This was due, as I frequently pointed out to Congressional committees, to the fact we were looting the next generation by bonds bearing interest, and I defined current democracy as the art of passing the buck to Providence and the bill to posterity.

Most of the activities of the People's Lobby during the Second World War were devoted to trying to get such domestic policies as would not give the lie extraordinary to our protestations of concern for the rest of the world. Each of the years we were admittedly fighting a war we held one or two conferences in Washington—sometimes fairly well attended, and usually quite fairly reported in the press—on the economic issues involved. The talks were printed as pamphlets, and 8,000 to 10,000 were sent our members, editors of papers and magazines, and church, labor, farm and civic leaders and libraries throughout the nation. They sold at only 10¢ or 15¢, with quantity rates. At all of the talks we had representatives of labor, farm, church or business organizations, and usually of some government agency.

In January 1942, we discussed "War Taxes and War Economics"; in February 1943, "Maximum Food for Rationing." In 1944, the two subjects discussed, with no holds barred, were "Shall It Be the Century of the Common Man or the Century of Cartel Control?" and "The People's Stake in War Production." The year of VE and VJ our two conferences were, in January, anticipating the early ending of "hot war," on "Some American Problems in 1945 and Suggested Solutions," at which we featured a talk by Harry D. White, Assistant Secretary of the Treasury on "International Monetary and Financial Cooperation"; and in June, following the birth of United Nations, on "The Economic and Social Council of the United Nations," at which all speakers recognized the paramount importance of this agency of the first international organization with even a modicum of joint military authority.

At this meeting Dr. Colston E. Warne quoted a recent statement of the Federal Council of Churches: "International economic co-operation is essential if the society of nations, torn by war and the lust for power, is to be knit together into an effective world community." That of course, precludes competitive profit grabbing, at home and abroad—which the Council hasn't yet dared fight.

The following month Dr. Warne in a nation-wide broadcast under the auspices of the Lobby, over the American Broadcasting Company, said:

"In the past, wide-spread unemployment has been cared for and the unemployed kept from violence by relief and by the more or less useful tasks of the WPA. It was financed by interest-bearing bonds running for 40 to 50 years.

"That isn't the American way, and we all know it. A large majority of our people realized it, long before Hitler's armies marched into Poland.

"Even adequate and inclusive unemployment insurance is, for any long period, not the answer, because failure to attain the maximum possible production lowers the standard of living below adequate levels, while maintaining an army of unemployed by taxes or bonds. This is just as much a dead loss as maintaining an equal army in uniforms. The cost falls on those who are producing.

"Congress, the Smaller War Plants Corporation, and the Department of Commerce have been framing a program to help little business become big business through subsidies and crutches from the cradle to the grave. They realize that about a third of small business ventures fail the first year, and only one out of five lives for ten years, and are seeking the remedy through the subsidy of cheap credit and governmental assistance.

"Even the fact that we spent nearly seven billion dollars for alcoholic drinks last year doesn't fully explain our mental state when we call this 'Private Enterprise.'

"To offset this outpouring of government help to large and small businesses, we are now spending in subsidies to consumers $2.5 billion a year to keep prices from rising further. This essential antidote to subsidized 'private enterprise' amounts to about four times the expense we incurred for consumer subsidies three years ago.

"The People's Lobby is attempting to stop some of these inflationary trends by securing a government investigation of the capital structure of corporations, which will probably reveal at least fifty billion of inflated stock valuations; also to secure legislation levying a special tax on the wartime increase in the selling prices of city and farm lands."

We stressed throughout the war the futility of expecting "peace" after the Axis Powers were knocked out, under the economic system of the "peace loving" nations. In May 1942, the Lobby's Board of Directors adopted the following statement on the war:

"The winning of the war by the nations committed to

democratic processes is our first concern. Assurance of an economic order which will minimize the danger of recurrence of armed conflict also is of vital importance. We concur in the recent pronouncement of the Executive Committee of the British Labor Party:

" 'It is now widely recognized that this war is not merely the outcome of the ambitions of two evil men; it is also the product of the circumstances which gave them power. It is widely recognized that circumstances which have given birth to two World Wars within a generation must be radically and speedily transformed. . . .

" 'The Labour Party asks that we register now, as a nation, our recognition that this war has already, socially and economically, effected a revolution in the world as vast, in its ultimate implications, as that which marked the replacemen of Feudalism by Capitalism. All over the world, the evidence is abundant that this revolution has deeply affected men's minds; our central problem is to discover its appropriate institutions, above all, if we can, to discover them by consent. . . .

" 'We have to choose now, because the character we give to the remaining period of this conflict itself determines the character of reconstruction, domestic and international.'

"Our pledges of a new order of economic justice, to follow this war, will fall on deaf ears unless we now achieve in America such subordination of private profits to the public good as will provide an earnest of our real post-war intent.

"The courage of our armed forces, the efficiency of our production machine and the brilliance of our military and civilian leadership will not of themselves avail to end the deep and widespread distrust peoples in conquered and threatened areas feel for Britain and for the United States.

"That distrust can best be ended and turned into active

cooperation by putting into practice at home now the principles of economic justice we are in danger of postponing for the duration. Such action would fortify the spirit of all on the fighting and the factory fronts."

In April 1943 Irving Brant, at the time Washington editorial writer for the *Chicago Sun-Times,* broadcast over the Blue Network, at one of our luncheons, the following indictment of our war program and policies—a record which helps explain some of our troubles since VE and VJ Days:

"The State Department must stop doing a wrong-way Corrigan every time a diplomatic pilot leaves the ground. We are losing the peace more slowly than we were a month ago, and three steps are necessary to blot out the effect of past blunders and to wipe out present doubt and indecision. The first step toward winning the peace is the same as toward winning the war. It is to open a second fighting front in Europe this year, and prove to Soviet Russia that she does not stand alone.

"The second step is to stop dallying with French, Spanish and Hungarian fascism, and make American diplomacy a living, breathing, fighting force for freedom and democracy.

"The third step is for the Senate to pass the Ball-Hatch-Hill-Burton resolution, or a suitable variant of it, and thus serve notice that after smashing the Axis we are not going to crawl back into our hole and await the coming of the Third World War.

"Postwar understanding with Russia must start on the field of battle. I am confident that the Continent will soon be invaded, but for a year and a half the Soviets have been fighting the war of liberation virtually alone.

"When doubt begins, it eats like a corrosive acid into the foundations of friendship. If the second front does not come this year, the shock to relations with the Soviets will be practically beyond repair. If Soviet Russia breaks the Nazi power unaided, you can write the western democracies off the map as far as the future of Europe is concerned.

"This does not mean that Russia, winning the war without our help, would proceed to overrun the Continent. No—the Continent would proceed to overrun Russia. Every little nation from the Baltic to the Black Sea would shout to Moscow: 'I'm your friend. I've always been your friend. Protect me against my neighbors.' The United States and Great Britain would be the men who weren't there.

"Soviet-American friendship was retarded by American military intervention against the Soviets in 1918, but had its foundations laid by American relief of the Russian famine in 1923, which helped disprove the Marx-Trosky doctrine that international revolution was needed to protect socialist states against capitalist neighbors.

"Long before we became Russia's ally in the war, the old suspicions were vanishing. Why is it, then, that all over Europe—in Russia, in Great Britain, in France, in Central Europe and the Balkans—a sudden fear is cropping out that the United States has become the friend of fascism? Why is it rumored that we are planning to build a chain of buffer states against the Soviets? The State Department, I am glad to say, has repudiated these reports. But why should it even be necessary to disavow so fatal a course?

"Because for five months we have kept fascist officials in power all over North Africa. Because for five months we have maintained, as resident general of French Morocco, the Nazi-minded General Nogues, the man who ordered French troops to fire on our American soldiers as they landed at Casablanca. Because we allow thousands of Spanish Republicans to rot in African concentration camps, while their fascist brethren walk whistling down the streets. Because

American diplomats sing the praises of the fascist dictator of Spain, who in turn sings the praises of Adolf Hitler. Because Tibor de Eckhardt, Hungarian satellite of the Hungarian satellites of Hitler, comes to the United States and is taken into the bosom of the State Department.

"Put all this together and you have a picture of American diplomacy turning to the fascists, the feudalists, the outgrown monarchists of Europe as the instruments through which we are to establish the four freedoms and the Atlantic Charter.

"I believe that neither President Roosevelt nor Secretary of State Hull has any intention of erecting buffer states against the Soviets. But policies are what they become in the hands of the human instruments chosen to put them into effect. Choose a man who fears democracy to deal with social discontent, and you have a denial of democracy.

"What we are suffering from in American diplomacy is fear of social unrest. This fear is translated into an administrative policy which destroys at the bottom what is planned at the top. It is a problem of State Department personnel, but it has a deeper negative root. There is no core of burning indignation in our diplomacy, no flaming zeal for human rights. We butter up fascists when we should be ramming the butter knife down their throats. The British Eighth Army marched 1,600 miles westward across Africa and left not a trace of fascism behind it. The American Army marched 900 miles eastward across Africa, and left fascism flourishing everywhere in its rear.

"If we are going to win the peace, now or at any time, we must deliver to political fascism the same terms that were handed at Casablanca to the fascist armies—unconditional surrender."

Of course we didn't do that—but backed them, then and

after the war, though executing some of their henchmen after the Nurnberg trials!

At the invitation of Mrs. Ann Hedgman, the efficient executive of the organization working for a permanent Fair Employment Practices Act, I went on their steering committee which met two or three times a month when the legislative situation on their bill was very tense. This included representatives of church, labor and civic organizations which realized that President Roosevelt's Commission to protect the rights of Negroes, set up by Executive Order after threats of a march on Washington, would be terminated as soon as the war danger passed.

Of course no legislation was enacted, for while the Negro is at least a semi-respectable citizen in most states of the Union (except the deepest south) when America's safety is at stake, in much of the nation he loses that immunity from malevolent ignorance when the danger seems to be past. The Negro is valued only when he is needed because of manpower shortage, and barring the few delirious years of preparation for the collapse of 1929, only in war economies has the Negro been—and, probably, will he be—an asset in American life, under our present economic system.

The President's Civil Rights Committee stated in its Report in 1947:

"In a world forever tottering on the brink of war, civil rights will be precarious at best. In a nation wracked by depression and widespread economic insecurity, the inclination to consider civil rights a luxury will be more easily adopted. We need peace and prosperity for their own sake; we need them to secure our civil rights as well."

One of the ablest members of that Committee stated to me privately—the only way it is safe to be intelligent in Washington: "We are just fooling the Negro when we hold out any hope of equality to him under the profit system."

In America, under that system, the best the Negro can hope for is less than equality in lack of economic opportunity in peace, and less than equality in lack of civil rights in war. Giving good Government jobs to able Negroes—the large number of whom is increasing rapidly—is not a solution, and will not help, except so far as it creates divine discontent. Voicing such views is not, however, conducive to large contributions for any organization.

Starting in 1944, the Lobby waged a continuous public discussion with the Treasury Department and the Bureau of Internal Revenue over the public scandal of permitting big corporations and other enterprises to spend vast sums in advertising, in no way connected with the sale of goods they normally manufactured—but some of which in the war economy they were not permitted to produce—and deducting the cost for tax purposes as a cost of doing business.

Advertising had increased in 1940 to 160% of the pre-war basis, and was around $2 billion, while by 1950, it had increased to about $5 billion, including newspaper, magazine and radio. Much of this was devoted to extolling "The American Way" and "free enterprise," and must have cost the Government several billion dollars over a few years, as the big outlay was by major concerns enriched by war contracts profits, while Government debt was increasing by billions yearly.

Needless to stress, we didn't get any help on this campaign from the patriotic papers and radio companies which got the advertising—in fact after the first publicity on the Treasury ruling that "propaganda" advertising was not deductible as a proper cost of doing business, we got very little radio time—Mutual and the very "liberal" Columbia Broad-

casting System refusing the Lobby a single spot—while newspaper publicity for our program was cut materially, though
the wire services, particularly the United Press, continued
their helpful cooperation.

Perhaps an additional explanation was that beginning in
1944 the Catholic press rode me pretty hard, for exposing
that the Catholic hierarchy controlled Congress, and prevented Federal aid to education because they couldn't get a
cut for their parochial schools.

People's Lobby took the position that separation of Church
and State is more really "The American Way" than permitting profiteering corporations to evade their taxes so as to
hang onto their war-depleted domestic markets through irresponsible advertising.

On September 5, 1946, after much prodding from us, Wm.
T. Sherwood, Acting Commissioner of Internal Revenue,
wrote us: "It may be stated generally that the cost of advertising may be deducted only when such advertising is designed to interest the public in the company or its products
with the object in view of producing a return commensurate
with the amount of such expenditure. Any cost of advertising space or time that is not designed to create such interest
or produce such result may not be deducted. It may also be
stated, generally, that sums of money expended for lobbying purposes, the promotion or defeat of legislation, and
the exploitation of propaganda, including advertising other
than trade advertising, are not deductible from gross income."

The Treasury's concern for consumers didn't last long
after business attacked this ruling. The U.S. Chamber of
Commerce started a big advertising campaign on "American
Opportunity," and other business splurges were put on after
assurances of liberal interpretations on tax deductions.

On November 22, 1946 we wrote the Bureau of Internal Revenue:

"1. Has the Treasury Department made any ruling which the U.S. Chamber of Commerce can interpret as a go ahead signal for their 'American Opportunity' campaign?

"2. Did big business interests put pressure on the Treasury Department and Congress not to tax war profits and personal incomes heavily, with the bait of 'free' advertising for bonds?"

On December 23, 1946 Commissioner Joseph D. Nunan wrote us: "With respect to your first question, you are advised that the Bureau will not discuss with, or disclose to, any person except the taxpayer or its duly authorized representative, the tax consequences of any transacton. You will appreciate, therefore, the Bureau may not divulge any information relative to the action taken or to be taken in regard to this matter.

"Your second question is not pertinent to the administration of the revenue system and it is not the policy of the Bureau to comment on such matters."(!)

And so the Treasury betrayed consumers, and our efforts to get Congress to act in the matter failed.

CHAPTER TEN

Hot War Passes into Cold War

Soon after VJ Day a Senator posed the question to me: "What are we going to do with all the officers after the war? Colonels won't want to go back to being soda jerkers." At the time there were about 630,000 commissioned and non-commissioned officers, and once about three years later there was one and a half colonels for every second lieutenant —a disparity of rank. Generals also need armies.

One of the tragic results of war, to a "victor," is that it breeds in the people of a strong and mechanized nation such confidence in the efficacy of force that they ignore the obvious alternative—such organization, domestic and international, as will reduce to a minimum the probability of recourse to force. A second result of an all-out war is the creation of a military caste, in which power, prestige and pay depend upon large numbers in the armed forces. The rapid demobilization of our armed forces after VJ Day was a shock to the higher echelons in all the armed services, few if any of whom have been zealots for the moral equivalent of war. They knew the "American Century" meant an armed camp. We now (1951) face a $65 billion to $70 billion a year arms and armament program.

When the early boom of the "New Deal" faded, Leon Henderson tried to calm the timorous souls who feared that capitalism was passing out with his classic remark, "There's lots of life in the old capitalist gal yet." Joseph P. Kennedy, early "New Deal" Ambassador to Great Britain, in his book "I'm For Roosevelt" published during the 1936 Presidential campaign, cited as a major reason that the selling price of stocks on the New York Stock Exchange had increased during Roosevelt's first term by some $37 billion. President Truman in his Budget Message in January 1947 also exposed the hypocrisy of pretending the "New Deal" had a consumer slant. He stated:

"It has always been the Government's duty to provide whatever assistance is required to afford private enterprise a chance to prosper." He was probably not aware of the implicit contradiction in describing the system of government underwriting of business as "private enterprise" or, like Roosevelt, never let the facts affect any action to which he was committed. President Truman attempted to justify his program of helping business to shift from hot war profiteering to cold war profiteering by citing the opening of the west in the nineteenth century as "a principal economic service of the Federal Government," and continued:

"Today our great new frontiers are in river valley developments, in air transport, in new scientific discoveries, and in the application of the new science and technology to human progress. These new frontiers can be developed only by the cooperation of Government and private enterprise." That cooperation in the past had pretty consistently consisted of assuring a big enough stake for success to keep speculators coming, and for several years a large part of the capital structure of corporations was provided by what Adolph A. Berle, in describing the fact, called "self-generating capital," that is corporate profits after ample dividends and moderate taxes, retained for business expansion.

This had been so extensive that the Securities and Exchange Commision reported early in 1945: "American industry as a whole is financially prepared to reconvert to peacetime production, and also to undertake considerable expansion, without recourse to outside sources of funds."

About the same time, Pearl Buck, who knows her Asia thoroughly, wrote in *This Month:* "The peoples of Asia today are more frightened than ever of Empire. They see the world of tomorrow committed to empire, not only to the empires they know, of Britain, France and Japan, but to potential new empires. One of them is the United States, our country, the nation that belongs to the American people. It is quite possible that we may be building an empire without knowing it."

Up to the end of 1944, the Reconstruction Finance Corporation and subsidiaries had made authorizations of $32.3 billion for war purposes, and disbursed over $18 billion. Early in 1945, R.F.C. Chairman Jesse Jones reported that "247 plants aggregating $3,100,000,000 are leased to operators at an annual rental of $1.00 a year. In these plants no charge is made to the government procurement agency for plants or plant facilities in the supply contracts. In the remaining 1,858 projects, in the amount of $4,900,000,000, rentals have been collected aggregating $422,000,000." This covered a number of years, and the plants were located in 46 states. Many of the contracts stipulated the Government must let the companies have first bid on the plants.

During World War Two, the Lobby tried without visible success to get contracts permitting the Government to retain plants and equipment which it financed, and after the war to have it hold such plant and equipment for production.

At the close of the war, "our" Government owned more convertible industrial plants than any other nation except Russia. They were the grand prize for industrial patriotism and, with billions of war surplus, went largely to the big owners of America. However industry, even during the closing days of the Hot War, was getting restive under the minimum controls government had imposed, and wanted to chart its own course and leave government to organize a war any time business methods made this appropriate.

A government which conscripts men and not money in war can't keep America out of war. Realizing this, People's Lobby in February 1946 held a Conference in Washington, with all Government agencies and Members of Congress invited to attend, on "America Needs an Over-All Plan," with spokesmen for consumers, the Federal Power Commission, War Assets Corporation, National Housing Agency, Department of Agriculture, National Commission for the Defense of Democracy through Education, and of transportation. We published and circulated, as usual, several thousand of the pamphlets with all the talks, and stated in the Foreword:

"Pandemonium production, even if mass production, is not a substitute for planned mass production. Rivalry among regional authorities, all subsidized out of the Federal Treasury and all competing for consumers' pocketbooks, is a throwback to three milk delivery companies operating on the same street—only more so!"

Three years later, in March 1949, the Congressional Joint Committee on the President's Economic Report, with only two members—Senator Taft and former Representative

Rich, of Pennsylvania, wholly dissenting—said in a long statement on economic conditions:

"The Government, which is the only instrumentality that can balance the needs of agriculture, industry, and labor, cannot afford to be without a plan. Industry plans for the years ahead, and counts among its executives some of the most efficient planners we have. Labor and agriculture likewise plan for the future, but none of these plans has any assurance of successful accomplishment unless they are geared one with another, and it is only the Government, as the representative of all groups, all classes, all callings, that can provide the framework, within which each separate group and class and calling can operate." Senator Joseph C. O'Mahoney was Chairman of this Congressional Joint Committee, but Congress completely ignored the Committee's challenge to intelligence and chart to peace!

The "Economic Stabilization Act of 1949" was supposed to be the answer to national planners' prayer, as its alleged purpose was "to encourage maximum production and supply"—but it did not commit the Government to do any of the things essential for a national plan. The bill definitely stipulated: "No plan shall contain any provision for the fixing of prices," and while authorizing priorities and allocations and general controls, stated: "but not including rationing at the retail level of consumer goods for household or personal uses." Such an Act did not become law till the aggression from North Korea had shown we must gear our economy to make force, temporarily at least, our reliance for having refused cooperation and world order.

In December of that year, in appreciation of the implications of the Marshall Plan, Sir Stafford Cripps, then Chancellor of the British Exchequer, said: "You cannot internationally plan unplanned economies: it is a contradiction in terms. Planning internationally, which is being so forcibly impressed upon us by our American friends, implies that the governments of the different countries must be able to carry out by direction, or by planning, the various requisites of the international plan, otherwise international planning of course falls to the ground." Sir Stafford realized direction is the essence of ownership.

The publicity on our conference on national planning, and the interest of our members, made the Board decide to devote most of our efforts to pamphleteering and publicity, though the Lobby appeared at six or seven hearings every year, or filed briefs, till it suspended operations late in 1950.

In January 1947, for the first time, People's Lobby elected a business man as President—James H. McGill, well-to-do manufacturer of Valparaiso, Ind., who had been an American "left-winger" ever since he read Henry George's "Progress and Poverty" and "Social Problems" in his early manhood. He had been an active supporter of the Lobby since it was organized and a Board member many years, and worked closely as President till his death, within two years.

Upon taking office, Mr. McGill issued a statement which was not designed to bring consolation to standpatters—and did not increase large contributions to the Lobby—including: "Reliance upon makeshift measures and subsidies to the victims of economic exploitation instead of ending economic exploitation is futile, and can only make inevitable changes, when they come, more drastic. Since Government has underwritten unemployment, Government must now underwrite employment, because Government underwriting of unemployment, without underwriting of employment through public ownership of natural resources, natural monopolies and basic industries, means demoralization of Government credit and nation-wide chaos."

In furtherance of Mr. McGill's thesis we held a Conference, in June of that year, on "Responsibility for Employment," also well publicized, with talks printed as a pamphlet. The breadth of our approach is shown by the fact the speakers included: Dr. Colston E. Warne, member of the Consumers' Advisory Committee to the President's Council of Economic Advisers and President of Consumers' Union —who stressed government's paramount responsibility; John Carson, Director the Cooperative League U.S.A. (later a member of the Federal Trade Commission); Kermit Eby, Director Education and Research, CIO; Dr. Emerson P. Schmidt, Director Research Department, U.S. Chamber of Commerce; Prentiss L. Coonley, Industrial Consultant; Dr. J. T. Sanders, Legislative Counsel of the National Grange; and Russell Smith, Washington Representative of the National Farmers' Union. Some of these spoke only personally. Talks by Messrs. Warne, Carson and Schmidt were broadcast by the National Broadcasting Company.

A very few of our members were a bit put out that we had a representative of the U.S. Chamber of Commerce on our broadcast, but we have always believed in giving all sides of a problem, so far as possible, so as to "prove all things" and then expect (or at least hope) that people would "hold fast that which is good." Authoritarianism has never been a plank in People's Lobby programs!

In May 1948, in recognition of the growing world turmoil, our Conference was on "World Planning or World Chaos," and our speakers all recognized the choice, though differing on methods to get world planning. The *Washington Post* story on the conference was captioned, "Thoughtful views on how to save the world from chaos." Speakers representing the viewpoints of their organizations included: the National Grange, American Veterans Committee, United

World Federalists, American Federation of Scientists, Public Affairs Institute, Congress of Industrial Organizations, Women's International League for Peace and Freedom, and People's Lobby.

The urgency of the choice was admirably put by Mr. Irving Panzer, speaking for the American Veterans Committee: "Either we create effective world government or we face a continuation of the international anarchy which can only lead to war. Not this year, not next year, perhaps not even this decade, but eventually, if the world finds no better defense against war than preparing for it, we face atomic war and chaos."

Since consumers' rights were being ignored by Congress, in 1949 our Conference was on "What Responsibility to Consumers Have Government, Industry, Farmers, Labor, Cooperatives?" with representatives of each speaking. In 1950 we issued a pamphlet "The Consumers' Program the 81st Congress Should Enact"—which Congress almost completely ignored—perhaps getting in training for its malevolent record in the First Session of the 82nd Congress, in 1951.

The Marshall Plan, Point Four and the concerted drive against civil rights were the main new concerns of the Lobby in the strange transition from hot to cold war, while we naturally opposed the ruthless selling of war surplus and war plants to the horde of exploiters who tried to get them for a song. A later chapter tells the story of how we tried to get church, labor and farm organizations to cooperate in urging international controls.

Late in 1946 we published an article, "Public Ownership of Coal Is Imperative," by the late Dr. Walter N. Polakov —whose authorship could not be revealed, because he was the head of the Research Department of the United Mine

Workers of America—and sent reprints out widely. Dr. Polakov noted the fact: "The economic loss from burning the chemical left in raw coal is many times the worth of the coal itself." And he concluded: "A National Resources Board should be created by Congress to direct the production and distribution of all the nation's natural resources; to plan their acquisition by the Government, and to administer them when acquired by the Government." This was of course anathema to John L. Lewis—and to most other labor leaders as well.

The Lobby backed the Registration of Lobbying Act of 1946, for the same reasons we had backed a similar plan when lobbying was being investigated by a Senate Committee, of which Thadeus H. Caraway was Chairman, in 1930. When an investigation of lobbies was suggested in 1949, however, we issued the following statement widely quoted: "To admit our stalwart legislators are so naive that they can be led to the slaughter by siren voices of finance and commerce makes a laughing stock of democratic processes. Such innocence deserves the protection of home influences at home, not a salary several times the average American family's, and lots of perquisites, in distant Washington.

"Fear of lobbyists is evidence either of the inadequacy of the platform upon which all Members of the House, and a third of the Senate, were elected last November, or complete lack of faith in that platform. The wiles of wine, women and song in making up the minds of Congress have been supplanted by the insidiousness of press, radio and television, but a man is a man for all that. To fortify Congressmen against lobbyists, Congress should do three things:

"1. Establish a school to put Congressmen wise to the wiles of would-be vote manipulators.

"2. Require public registration of stocks and bonds, and of land not actually used by them, which Congressmen own.

"3. Pass a law requiring all campaign contributors to sign a release to parties and individual Members of Congress from any implied obligation, so both may be free to vote and work for the welfare of all the American people."

The chief fear of People's Lobby about the Marshall Plan was that it might be perverted, as it was, into an effort to turn the economic clock back in Europe.

Witnesses at Congressional Committee hearings are not permitted to ask questions of Committee members. Instead of appearing at the Marshall Plan hearings we therefore wrote Sen. Arthur H. Vandenberg, at the time Chairman of the Senate Committee on Foreign Relations—and an eminently wise and fair statesman—asking whether the Government intended to underwrite the profits or losses of Americans selling goods to European countries to favor large American concerns; or to oppose construction of factories, the output of which might later compete for markets with American factories. Senator Vandenberg replied, about the European Recovery Program:

"There will be *no* guarantee of either the capital or the profits (or the losses) of these investments. The *only* agreement is that the Government of the United States will guarantee ultimate convertibility of any such funds into American dollars. Meanwhile, any such investments of private funds will be deducted from the total ERP figures.

"I would expect ERP to make its purchases in America on the best available basis regardless of the size of the bidder. I should hope that—all things being equal—every effort would be made to distribute these purchases over as large as possible a sector of American industry.

"I can respond categorically that there is no intention to

'discriminate' in the administration of ERP in the fashion you indicate. The *sole* objective is to make Western Europe self-sustaining and I expect ERP to be administered in this spirit."

The Secretary of State, in reply to our question whether socialization of industry would be opposed under E.R.P., had in October 1947 written us:

"The first general report of the Committee of European Economic Co-operation contains no provisions or discussions relating to the socialization of the means of production and distribution within the participating countries.

"There has been no United States policy established which would oppose any step toward socialization which those countries might, by democratic means, determine. In the past, this Government has not questioned the right of any other country to nationalize or otherwise affect the ownership of property located within the jurisdiction of that country.

"The Government has, however, insisted that there should be prompt, effective and adequate compensation for American property rights affected by any such action."

We, of course, gave wide publicity to both statements.

Our following letters to the Secretary of State and to Hon. John Kee, Chairman the House Committee on Foreign Affairs, about Point Four, shows how we welched on our pledges to Europe:

"Our record in Germany since V.E. day goes far to explain the appeal of desperation which extremists make to undeveloped countries throughout the world. In the *Nation,* November 26, 1949, Carolus, the pseudonym of its correspondent in West Germany, writes:

" 'A vast majority of the German people—not only the Social Democrats but all of German labor, including the workers organized in Catholic unions—have openly demanded the nationalization of key industries. They cannot envision either a democratic or a peaceful Germany if these industries remain in private hands.

" 'The preservation of the status quo will mean that the same powerful financial interests which have two world wars and the Hitler regime on their conscience will become the masters of the new state. The opposition of these interests to the Socialist reorganization of the German economy which is the precondition of real democracy is reinforced by the admonition of the United States: Germany must be made safe for private enterprise.'

"In the *New Republic,* November 28, 1949, Percy Winner, its Foreign Affairs Editor, writes:

" 'The Rhineland's coal-and-steel heavy industry used to be dominated by seven great Konzerns. Now there are fourteen "industrial units." The men in charge, however, are the same as those who practised the *Herr im Hause* system under the Kaiser, under Weimar, under Hitler: Kost in coal, Dinkelbach in steel, Henle, Bruns, Viet, Reusch, Zangen, Pferdmenges and others equally—and unpleasantly—familiar.

" 'Thanks to the efficiency of these "masters-in-the-house" —and no one who had any experience with the German war machine in either of the two wars can doubt their efficiency—Western Germany's steel production rose sharply during the first half of 1949.

" 'They worked under some handicaps, since the passing fancy of the political masters, the Western high commissioners, made cartels unpopular—a lamentable but not irreparable difficulty. In the past, under Weimar for example, they had faced and overcome similar handicaps, learning how to interpret the will rather than the word of official decrees. This time too, they guessed—and apparently accurately—that the political masters weren't really eager to shackle an industrial production so necessary for the supreme purpose of all politics—war, of course.

" 'So they resorted to the *Frühstückskartelle;* they made "gentleman's agreements" at pleasant business luncheons. The trend, they knew, was in their favor. The old, enormously powerful German Manufacturers Association was coming to life once more at Köln under the charmingly ambiguous title, Committee for Economic Questions.

" 'There was nothing unclear, however, about the fact that the Committee grouped 32 economic associations which control about 90 percent of Western German's industrial production. Nor did they mistake the meaning of the desire of their American Associates to have *Gesetz-75* changed to prevent any of the property confiscated and held by the Western Allies from being nationalized.'

"A United Press dispatch from Berlin, December 3rd, 1949, quotes Walter Reuther, President United Automobile Workers, CIO, as telling a press conference there that the Americans and British have put back into power in the Ruhr 'the very people who helped Hitler to office and helped him to wage war. There is a trend toward re-establishing the old control groups. This is a very real threat to German democracy and world democracy.' He said the American and British veto of a German proposal to nationalize the Ruhr coal mines should be rescinded, and that 'nationalization would be the best guarantee that Ruhr production would not be war production.'

"The three charges cited, if even substantially true—and the authors, and both the *Nation* and the *New Republic,* are responsible people in position to get the facts—are a serious indictment of our policy in Germany. Before we submit these charges to the Committees of Congress directly or by implication responsible for America's foreign policies, and ask they investigate them, we would like to have your comments."

Both letters were formally acknowledged.

The Senate Committee on Foreign Relations accorded me about six minutes at their hearing on Point Four, where representatives of the Federal (now National) Council of Churches, American Veterans' Committee, Friends Legislative Committee and other organizations approved the principle but deplored the small amount of the principal involved—some $35 million. Nearly all of them urged that Point Four be administered exclusively by the United Nations.

It will manifestly be hard to convince the over two-billion non-U.S. Americans in the world that we are really trying to raise their standard of living when we spend less than one thousandth as much on this as on arms and armaments.

The Nixon bill to outlaw Communists, but not the Communist Party, was given lengthy hearings by the House Committee on Un-American Activities, and I tried repeatedly to be allowed to testify against it, but without success. Finally late in June 1950 I filed the following brief, to be incorporated in the hearings:

"This bill is one of the most subversive and futile efforts to create a crime, instead of directly outlawing the Communist Party, since that seems to be the purpose. It should be noted that the bill gives, by inference, approval of a homebrew 'totalitarian dictatorship,' since it makes it illegal to work for such, 'the direction and control of which is to be vested in, or exercised by or under the domination or control of, any foreign government, foreign organization, or foreign individual.' Mr. Nixon evidently believes in a protected market.

"If the Communist Party is legal, it is subversive of both intelligence and of law to try to make scapegoats of those acting as or for a party, unless they commit a crime.

"This Committee should ask the Supreme Court, at once, for an advisory opinion on the constitutionality of the bill, and the Supreme Court might appropriately tell you what parts of the Constitution should be repealed or amended to make the bill constitutional. The Court might also, in more judicial language than I can command, tell you that inflation is a greater threat to America's well being than the communists, backs or fronts, and that if any government agency hasn't discovered employees who have betrayed their country, or attempted to, and prosecuted them, the chiefs of such agency should be relieved of office for inefficiency.

"Just as we are learning that finessing, to use a bridge term, is sometimes more effective in a cold war than force, we are also learning that ending internal conditions which produce believers in or advocates of extreme measures is much more efficacious than increasing the list of acts or failures to act punishable by incarceration, fine, or economic or physical death.

"There is a widespread feeling in America that much of the alarm over communists is a cover-up for alarm about economic conditions here, over which communists have no control. The greater the scare about communists, the easier it is to get billions for jobs producing armaments, which the people condone, while they would rebel against such expenditures for constructive domestic purposes.

"The military hierarchy in America owe a great debt of gratitude to communists here and abroad, whose activities keep them in power, while an efficient government would evolve policies which would greatly reduce the attempted justification for the military splurge. Our inane foreign policies have also helped communist activities, but suppressing communist sympathisers won't end our domestic or foreign policies.

"Your Committee in the past has been markedly tolerant of subversive activities of American cartellists who doubtless are sizeable contributors to both major parties. In May 1947 we wrote the President asking whether Americans found guilty of the practices for which German industrialists were about to be tried could be punished and July 29 of that year Ass't. Attorney General John F. Sinnot wrote us in reply to our question:

" 'The basic charges contained in the pending cartel indictments in Germany are not comprehended by existing legislation in the United States. To that extent, therefore, the only recourse is to Congress.'

"We promptly sent copies of our correspondence on this kind of subversive activities, with the President, and the State and Justice Departments, to the then Chairman of your Committee J. Parnell Thomas, asking the Committee investigate and draft legislation to meet the conditions, and giving a list of informed witnesses. Mr. Thomas replied that he had read the correspondence and would refer the matter to the Committee, but repeated requests to your Committee to act have been bi-partisanly ignored.

"It is notorious that your Committee, so anxious to save America from control by a foreign state, has ignored the fact the Vatican has for centuries tried to dominate the world, not by armed forces, but by a cold war, capitalizing inherent fear of the unknown hereafter, to get obedience to its earthly reaction, and it is probably the most corrupt and reactionary state in the world. Stalin doubtless borrowed the idea of the cold war from the Vatican, but he never sank so low as to pretend to determine what would happen to people after death.

"If Mr. Nixon is sincere in his fear of attempted overthrow of our Government by a foreign state, he would treat Catholics as he does Communists. There should be parity of treatment in a country where all people are supposed to be equal before the law. For full information your Committee can call on Paul Blanshard, author of 'American Freedom & Catholic Power,' and Avro Manhattan, author of 'The Vatican in World Politics.'

"We suggest again your Committee get an advisory opinion on the Nixon bill from the Supreme Court, because America doesn't want to be stamped a Fascist nation in the eyes of the world. Also, to prove the purity and patriotism of your efforts to save America, your Committee might ask immediate action by Congress to require every Federal employee getting over $3,000 salary to file a sworn statement of stocks and bonds he and his family own, corporations or enterprises with which they are or have been within the past three years connected in any way, and land and other real estate they own, except what they use personally."

A few months before this I met Dr. J. B. Matthews who had been in charge of investigations for the Committee, and whom I had known for about a quarter of a century, and told him I was surprised the Committee hadn't investigated me, as I tried to get it to do so. He replied: "Martin Dies (the first Committee Chairman) wanted to investigate you and have you as a witness, but I told him you would make a monkey of the Committee."

"You are no friend of mine," I came back, to which he retorted: "I might be a friend of yours, but I was getting a good salary from the Committee to protect them!" So the

Committee didn't get a chance to ride me, and I didn't get the chance to deride the Committee.

When William Benton was in charge of the Voice of America in the State Department, we had some vigorous correspondence, and I asked him to invite representatives of labor, church, farm, civic, and "radical" organizations to prepare statements of their views on domestic and international problems, to be "voiced" abroad by the Voice's staff. He turned it down cold, and expressed complete disagreement with my statement that America is the great counter-revolutionary. He wrote me that he, as I am, is a son of a foreign missionary and he seemed to think the "old time religion" was going to keep the peace.

Finally I wrote him, July 25, 1950 (when he was a U.S. Senator): "Permit me to suggest some of the facts about the United States—which the leaders of every nation in the world know—which we must change before it is worth while blowing in a lot of money to tell the world how noble we are—although we are not as vicious as some Russian broadcasts would make us out, and Russia does plenty of wholly inexcusable things.

"Here are some of our situations and practices we must change, because they make the world fear we shall try to dominate it:

"1. We have about 4,000,000 too many people trying to make a living in times of peace, for our economic system, including surplus marginal farmers, coal miners, railroad workers, excess personnel in government jobs etc., while war provides a way of getting 'full employment.'

"2. We are complete hypocrites in calling our economic system 'private enterprise,' because big and little business, farmers, and labor all ask a government handout or intervention in one form or another.

"3. Both New Deal and Fair Deal have repudiated the Democratic Party's alleged principle—ending special privileges—and instead have entrenched them, but tried to bribe the victims into acquiescence, through subsidies and 'social security' legislation—so property income has soared, and taxes haven't.

"4. We have deficiteered almost continuously for 20 years, making us a threat to small nations, who know that spells aggression.

"5. The sun never sets on Americans' investments, concessions, and military or naval bases, which creates the fear we shall revert to the doctrine, where the American dollar or uniform is, there is American territory.

"6. We have broken faith in Europe, China and Malaya, and backed reactionaries and fascists and opposed social ownership in Europe—though we agreed not to.

"7. We have used the slogan 'The American Century'— and major programs for future investment envision and advertise 'breathtaking' profits.

"8. Our Government or private citizens are grabbing all the natural resources throughout the world they can locate, directly or through preclusive buying.

"9. Advertising has degenerated into an apology for exploitation and a device by which industry may cheat the Government of taxes, to extol the system of private profits.

"10. We have ignored every basic proposal for the international controls of investments, natural resources and markets—essential to world prosperity and world peace.

"11. Only the billions Government now spends on the cold war, and on 'defense'—so largely wasted—prevents a collapse of our economy.

"12. Government policies have in the past 17 years cut the value of the dollar almost in half—the crooked way of making the poor pay more than their share of Government costs.

"What do you propose to do to change this record?"

The letter was not acknowledged, and so far as I know was not beamed to the four quarters of the world, though I submit it would have been as fair a statement as some that are used.

My letter was written just a month after the aggression across the 38th Parallel in Korea, and now, thanks to that action, there are only 2,000,000 unemployed in America. But a nation is never safe when it lives in mortal dread that total and indivisible peace may break out!

CHAPTER ELEVEN

The Fight for Consumers

In 1921 Senator George W. Norris introduced a bill to create a Government Marketing Corporation, empowered to buy farm products in the United States, process them and sell them here and abroad, the Directors being authorized to use producers' and consumers' cooperatives and to foster their development. The Corporation was to be given wide latitude, and of course the meat packers, big chain food stores and many retailers opposed it violently, and it was not even reported out of the Senate Committee on Agriculture, to which referred. It would have facilitated international organization of agriculture.

Soon after election in 1922, Senator Lynn J. Frazier of North Dakota, with the approval of Senator Norris, who was giving more time to public power, introduced the Norris bill with slight modifications, and Representative James H. Sinclair, also of North Dakota, introduced it in the House. Both major parties were afraid of it, and for over a decade

we couldn't get a hearing in the Senate, and never got one
in the House.

The "New Deal" with its Agricultural Adjustment Administration took people's minds off economics and diverted
them to makeshifts and short-term palliatives, as was intended. Efficiency has never been the easily besetting indul-
gence of democracies.

Big landed farmers worked for three substitutes for an
intelligent farm marketing program which protected consumers—the McNary-Haugen bill, the Agricultural Adjustment Administration, and farm parity prices. During the
Harding, Coolidge and Hoover administrations, farm spokesmen plugged for the McNary-Haugen bill, under which
farmers would pool the major farm products, for the domestic consumption of which they were paid a stipulated price,
while the export surplus was to be sold at the world price
and the loss assessed upon producers in proportion to their
sales in the domestic markets.

The bill was passed by Congress twice, but vetoed by
President Coolidge. It was the first admission by farmers
that their independence was over, and they couldn't be
helped by a protective tariff but needed Government organization of their selling. It was a forerunner of the "New
Deal" plan for the Agricultural Adjustment Administration
and parity prices for farm products, to enable farm producers
to exploit consumers as heavily as manufacturers exploit
them! Both plans wholly ignored domestic consumers, and
the need for world organization of agricultural production
and marketing as set up by the International Wheat Agreement in 1948—with all major nations, except Russia and
Argentina, included.

In 1926 Gardner Murphy, editor of the *Iowa Homestead*
(later merged with its rival, *Wallace's Farmer*) had stated

in an article in *The New Republic* that the American Farm
Bureau Federation and National Grange, and to only a
lesser extent the Farmers' Union, were controlled by banking and landed farmers.

Soon after Henry A. Wallace became Secretary of Agriculture in 1933, he stated in a speech at one of the Lobby's
luncheons in Washington, with a nation-wide broadcast,
that speculation in farm land was worse than the plague,
and almost as bad as war. I taxed him, privately, with hypocrisy—since, and he admitted it, the Administration's farm
program was directly designed to maintain and increase
speculation in farm land and farm land prices. He was in
politics, however, as he remarked to me on more than one
occasion, and he stayed there.

Hearings were finally granted in 1937 by the Senate Agriculture Committee on the Farm Marketing bill, at which
the first Consumers' Counsel in the U.S. Department of
Agriculture, Dr. Frederic C. Howe and his assistant, Gardner Jackson, endorsed its objective and Dr. Howe warned
that, desirable as producers' and consumers' cooperatives
are, they could not alone cope with the financial giants in
meat packing, milling, milk products, and distribution. The
Department of Agriculture opposed it, but the bill was
shortly thereafter voted out by the Committee, though it
died a pre-determined death on the Senate Calendar.

In 1933, early in his hectic career as Assistant Secretary
of Agriculture, Dr. Rexford G. Tugwell started his courageous fight to amend the Pure Food and Drugs Act to make
the administration thereof a positive protection for consumers instead of a brilliant locking of the stable door after
the mule was stolen—i.e., after consumers had been poisoned
or injured by chemicals or deleterious food ingredients.

At a hearing of The Senate Committee—of which Dr.

Royal G. Copeland, Senator from New York, and former Health Commissioner of New York City, was Chairman—I urged Mr. Tugwell's bill be approved, but amended to give the Pure Food and Drug Administration power to require all manufacturers to prove every claim they made for their products, and also authority to test every chemical and forbid its use, if deleterious.

Dr. Copeland admitted this would be legal, but said it was impractical politically. I reminded him the Democratic Party was in complete control of both branches of Congress, and what he was saying was that the party was the prisoner of profit-seeking and irresponsible interests. He couldn't deny it, so evaded the charge.

William Allen White, "the sage of Emporia" (Kansas), in an article about Dr. Tugwell and his fight to protect consumers from poisoned foods and drugs, wrote in an article in the *Washington Sunday Star,* Jan. 7, 1934:

"He must keep his control by his own attitude, his own policy, his own strategy, his own appeal to the American people. The most dubious struggle he will have will be to strengthen the Food and Drug Act. Many American newspapers and magazines think this act menaces the advertising of foods and drugs. They will not break with the President in other matters, but will oppose legislation which they feel will curtail advertising. Yet many people feel that the righteousness of the Tugwell measure, which prohibits fraudulent or misleading advertising, cannot be questioned. But to force a fight with the press on the Tugwell measure, at this time, may be bad politics." When isn't it!

Incidentally, the public can't expect to get the truth in newspapers—any more than in radio, fabrics, drugs or food —until they are willing to pay the cost of producing newspapers, instead of letting the advertisers pay so much of it.

On behalf of a small group of peace organizations I also presented a program of international co-operation to Secretary of State Cordell Hull, Chairman of our delegation at the 1933 International Economic Conference in London, designed to raise consumers' standards everywhere.

Mr. Hull was not a radical in any sense of the term, but knew when he had been left out on a limb. He was very indignant at the duplicity of President Roosevelt in putting through domestic policies which would effectively block international action, and said to me: "The President has asked me to get some sort of international agreement, but has taken action at home which makes it impossible for me to do so." I found the delegates from several other nations at this Conference agreed with him.

Although Secretary Hull booted Raymond Moley home from the London Conference, it was worse than "might as well not have been." It was a calamity, because it convinced the leaders of nations we now call "free" that we wouldn't stand for any measures which threatened our world supremacy. The failure was a feather in Hitler's hat.

In the winter of 1934, Dr. William Wirt of Gary, Ind., started riding the alleged radicalism of the "New Deal." Dr. Tugwell was soon transferred to working on Resettlement projects—where he did a good job, under the circumstances.

In the 82nd Congress fifteen years later, a House Select Committee on Chemicals in Foods, with Hon. John J. Delaney of New York Chairman, investigated the same issues as the Senate Committee under Chairman Copeland, and will probably be as futile, unless backed by consumers.

The selling price of farm lands had increased some 27 billion dollars during the first World War decade, 1910 to 1920, slumped, and started up again. It increased about $20 billion during World War Two. The U.S. Bureau of Agricultural Economics reported that in the nine years 1927 to 1935, rent for farms (chiefly land rent) paid to non-farmer landlords was $7,417 million, and though in 1932 it was only $582 million in three of the nine years it was over $1,000 million and in one year $1,110 million.

We tried to get Secretary Wallace to face the fact that since he admitted speculation in farm lands was a catastrophe, he should do something about it; but in June 1933 he wrote me, "The selling price of farm land reflects what farmers in their desire for land and homes are willing to pay for them"; though no one knew better than he that, as I promptly replied to him, "they pay what they have to."

By mid 1935, the selling price of farm lands had increased under the "New Deal's" first two years by a third or two-fifths, so I wrote him again, asking whether he intended to bring farm lands of the middle west up to the level of 1926, as he was trying to bring up farm prices. Dr. Mordecai Ezekiel, one of the bright lights among "New Deal" economists, replied:

"As you know, the AAA has no direct interest in the price of land. However, you no doubt also know that exceedingly low prices of land reflect the low level to which farm prices fell during the depression, and the fact that land values are rising is apparently the normal response to somewhat better economic conditions among farmers. The AAA Act still contains the provision that the objective of the Secretary is to establish parity levels at which the price of farm products is as high but no higher than the price of products farmers buy."

This was a complete admission that consumers were to be left out of the picture, and landed farmers were to be helped by Government to exploit consumers, just as mercilessly as manufacturers exploited them, through the strange device of "parity" for farm products—that is, parity of manufacturers and farmers in gouging consumers!

Both Dr. Howe, as Consumers' Counsel in the U.S. Department of Agriculture, and Gardner Jackson his assistant, tried to help consumers by issuing a *Bulletin* on prices, and organizing groups over the nation to stimulate consumer interest and action; but when they vigorously opposed the greed of both producers and processors of farm products, they were quickly frozen out of their jobs by President Roosevelt and Secretary of Agriculture Wallace. Donald Montgomery, who succeeded Dr. Howe—and later became Consumers' Counsel for the United Automobile Workers of America—tried valiantly to keep up the pace set when the office was created, but was boxed in, and given practically no funds on which to operate.

I appeared frequently at committee hearings of both branches of Congress on Housing, Taxation, and other consumer problems, but could merely make the record.

Complete disregard of consumers' rights was shown in the compact between industry and labor, announced at a meeting early in the war to quarantine aggressors, called by the U.S. Chamber of Commerce, at which its President, Mr. Eric Johnston, William Green, President A.F.L., and Philip Murray, President C.I.O., announced the labor-industry agreement. When the time for questions came, I asked: "Has the Department of Justice approved this conspiracy against consumers?" Not one of the three made any kind of response, but after I asked a second time a prominent business man, referring to my question, stated he thought some assurance should be given that the consumers would have some representation in any agency set up by the labor-management combination. This was not done, however.

To Mr. Johnston's great credit, when President Truman

appointed him Economic Stabilizer after the war in Korea started, he adopted and kept the consumers' viewpoint, and with courage and vigor repeatedly denounced the rapacity of organized labor, organized farmers and organized industry.

In February 1943 the Lobby held a conference in Washington on "Maximum Food Rationing," with the Chairmen of the House Committees on Agriculture and on National Defense Migration, and representatives of the U.S. Department of Agriculture, National Grange and National Farmers' Union as speakers.

While Harry S. Truman was Chairman of the Senate Committee Investigating War Programs we tried several times to get him to act to prevent the inevitable post-war results of war policies.

In April 1943, we wrote him: "Your Committee has rendered notable service to the American people, in exposing and correcting some of the inefficiency and graft inherent in the current practice of duplicating Government authority, diffusing it, and then diluting it. You can give an even larger service.

"Assistant Attorney General Tom C. Clark emphasized the need for this in his speech last week to the American Business Congress when, reporting that 100 mammoth corporations have gotten 'the great bulk of the $14,000,000,000 worth of new plants built at government expense,' he stated:

" 'Some of these corporations demanded and secured the right after the war to buy and control these new facilities constructed at government expense.'

"This convicts corporations which refused to produce needed war equipment, except on their terms, of at least moral treason, and government officials responsible, of almost criminal negligence. Will your Committee promptly investigate and make public the exact hold-up terms under which these 100 corporations agreed not to sabotage the war program?

"Under their plan, we shall have at the end of the war a full fledged fascist corporative state, a fact which the Dies Committee to investigate un-American activities chooses to ignore. This program of American industrial fascists would establish a form of industrial homesteading for private monopolies.

"We ask that your Committee request the Attorney General to cancel all such agreements to alienate government property, made under duress. These great aggregations of capital have no more legal right to third-degree Government than the police have to third-degree their prisoners, whether innocent or guilty. These traitorous corporations, some now in cahoots with agencies of enemy governments, must not be permitted to wreck our war and peace programs through the connivance of knock-kneed government officials. This is supposed to be a people's war."

To this, Hugh Fulton, Chief Counsel, replied May 8th: "Senator Truman has asked me to thank you for your letter of April 29 concerning the possible control after the war of government-built plants by large corporations. You may be assured that your suggestions will receive the careful consideration of the Committee."

Referring to this reply, we wrote Truman on May 11th: "In view of the entrenching of these great corporations, and the menace thereof, I respectfully ask that your Committee act on this matter at the earliest possible moment. Mr. Emil Rieve, President of the Textile Workers Union of America, at its biennial convention starting yesterday in New York, said on this subject:

" 'We have built these plants to benefit all the people of

the United States. They can do this job in peace as well as in war. They can do the job if the government keeps them and operates them as it operates the Tennessee Valley Authority. Labor must start to plan now for the kind of postwar world that it wants, and I think we all know the essentials.'

"I am sending our original letter to you, with Mr. Fulton's reply, to leaders of labor, church, farm and civic organizations over the country, who I know will be interested, and to the press of these organizations. The enclosed advertisement of a 'Victory Bull Market' from 'Poor's Investment Advisory Service' shows the urgency of our request."

No labor, church, farm, or civic organization took up the cudgels for consumers, and their press largely ignored the issue—so nothing was done—though Chief Counsel Fulton wrote us May 14: "Senator Truman has asked me to acknowledge your letter of May 11th urging again an investigation of agreements governing the construction and operation of Government-owned plants."

On June 5th and August 27th, we again jogged the memory of the Chief Counsel, but our files do not show any reply. A political investigator always knows what *not* to investigate.

In April that year, at our request, Senator George Aiken, Republican of Vermont, a member of the Senate Committee on Agriculture, went over the head of its Chairman, "Cotton Ed" Smith, of South Carolina, and arranged two hearings of the Committee on consumers' problems, at which representatives of half a dozen consumers' organizations and cooperatives appeared to suggest measures to protect consumers against higher prices and lower quality of goods.

In June, the group in the House known as "Friends of the Consumer" held a day's Conference in the House Caucus

Room, at which some 225 delegates of labor unions, cooperative and consumers' organizations asked for strengthening of O.P.A. and urged that roll-back subsidies be increased to prevent rapidly rising prices. At that Conference, Dr. Hartley A. Cross presented the program of Consumer's Union, which included:

"Congress should authorize the government to seize the plants and the materials of manufacturers, processors, etc., who strike against the national welfare by refusing to produce and distribute goods and commodities unless ceilings are pierced, quality standards destroyed, or exorbitant profits guaranteed. The no-strike policy should be extended to all producers who blackmail the government and the people by withholding commodities and goods from normal channels for consumption."

On behalf of the People's Lobby, I urged our program, which included having the Government *at once* take over processors and distributors of farm products, making them agencies of the Government, with equipment pooled and profits strictly limited, as in Britain, and also pointed out that the chief effect of roll-back subsidies was to increase the selling price of farm lands already dangerously high, and swell the profits of people in the food business. No other organization would back this program, and Consumers' Union has never pressed its program, although practically all handlers of foods tried to break through the price ceiling set in World War Two, or to have them increased.

The constant sniping of predatory business and its stooges in Congress at the Office of Price Administration forced Leon Henderson out of office as Price Administrator and scared Chester Bowles. In the summer of 1945, when the barrage of criticism was heaviest, we wrote Mr. Bowles urging he take a more aggressive position and advocate some measure like the Norris-Frazier-Sinclair Government Marketing Corporation, or at least more public markets. He replied:

"Our enforcement task is, perhaps, the greatest ever undertaken by a federal agency, and the staff available to us is small. I know that we can count on these enforcement officers to do more than their share in protecting honest businessmen and the general public against the wartime chiseler and the profiteer. Our efforts have the full backing of the Treasury Department and other federal agencies.

"The final test on whether the black market will be kept under control or whether it will grow to dangerous proportions, rests with the general public itself. The final complete answer to our black markets will come from the righteous indignation of our businessmen and from the general public."

Mr. Bowles' sincerity and ability are unquestioned, but his answer is typical of the thinking of pre-atomic-energy-release days. The assumption that people should go without necessities of life to prevent being looted by profiteers and black markets makes a mockery of government. A Government which cannot protect its people against black market aggressors at home can't identify real aggressors abroad.

Early in 1946, we suggested to Wilson Wyatt, Housing Expediter in the Office of War Mobilization and Reconversion, that he press for legislation to empower the government to operate plants to manufacture building materials and to refuse help for housing, where state and local governments failed to reduce the tax rate on buildings and increase it on land values—as several states had done.

The idea was not original, as Mrs. Eleanor Roosevelt had stated at a meeting of the Public Housing Association in Washington, in the winter of 1933–34, that the slow progress of public and other housing was due to speculation in land, profiteering in building materials and high labor costs; and Thurman Arnold as Assistant Attorney General had tried to break up the labor and material trusts—though he was fired for his honesty. The Lobby had urged our program at several Congressional Committee hearings.

Mr. Wyatt replied in February: "After a thorough study of all the proposals that have been made to deal with the housing emergency, I feel that my program embodies the proposals which will make it possible to do the job most effectively and most quickly. There have been a number of suggestions for making basic changes in our tax structure to discourage the speculation in land.

"Legislation either at the national or local level would be required to place these changes in effect and I am sure that this would take considerable time. I feel, therefore, that we should concentrate our energies in putting over the emergency program and then, when it is under way, work out with the Congress a permanent national housing policy."

He missed the boat, for with his great prestige he had a chance and wouldn't take it, but followed the adage of Turkey under the Sultans: "Never do today what you can put off till tomorrow." The fate of Turkey under the Sultans has a lesson, even for American procrastinators.

The National Security Act of 1947 creating the National Security Resources Board specifically states: "It is the intent of Congress to provide a comprehensive program for the future security of the United States." When Congress repealed most of the slight safeguards for consumers, it seemed to us this Act might be invoked to get something for them, and I wrote the Chairman, Hon. Arthur M. Hill, in August 1948. Two days later he replied, quoting my questions: "The National Security Resources Board has no power or authority 'to restore price-fixing and rationing for essential foods and other goods', or 'to allocate natural resources and material in short supply', or 'to impose restrictions on consumer credits', or 'to allocate credit to business enterprises so as to reduce unnecessary investment'." It was our try to make consumer security rate as part of "national security"!

At two annual meetings of Consumers' Union I tried to get it to put on a campaign to have the Bureau of Standards test and report on goods to all American consumers, as the Union does so effectively for its members; but they did not think it practicable.

In June 1949, on the eve of one of our conferences on consumers' problems, in Washington, I wrote Dr. Edward U. Condon, Director of the National Bureau of Standards, asking to be informed "whether the Bureau has facilities to test goods, clothing, cars, etc. such as Consumers' Union has, whether under the law you can publicize the facts developed, and whether you have funds to make such facts widely available to consumers."

Dr. E. C. Crittenden, Associate Director, replied: "Referring to your first question regarding facilities to test goods, clothing, cars, etc., this Bureau has a considerable amount of such facilities; and a considerable part of our work is related to such tests. Many tests of materials are made in connection with Government purchases, but even more work is done on the development of reliable and significant methods and apparatus for testing, which can be used by other laboratories as well as our own.

"Your second question is whether under the law we can publicize the facts developed. The statutory provisions under which this Bureau operates are very meager, being principally those enacted when the Bureau was established in 1901. Among those provisions is one that the Director 'may issue, when necessary, bulletins for public distribution, containing such information as may be of value to the public. . .' Under this very general authorization the Bureau has issued a great many publications giving general information about materials and methods of determining their properties. So far as the law is concerned we could include in such publications results of tests made on goods purchased by the Government.

"As to availability of funds to make information widely available to consumers, there are various ways by which this might be accomplished. One method which we already use for such information as we can supply is to publish circulars of information. The Bureau also supplies articles to trade journals and periodicals of interest to consumers. Both of these activities might be expanded if means were available to support a larger staff engaged in this kind of work.

"For several reasons it has never seemed wise to report results of tests made on goods purchased by the Government, because they are made on small samples, and may not have relation to the general product of a given manufacturer. Even more difficulty would be involved in making sure that the samples tested represented the products available to the general buying public. If this Bureau were to issue reports on products of a given kind, it would be under pressure to cover not only competing products of the same kind, but others as well.

"Since your letter refers particularly to organizations such as Consumers' Union, we must point out the difference between the status of such organizations and a Government bureau, especially one with such a reputation as the National Bureau of Standards has. Consumers' Union renders a highly valuable service, particularly to its members. A favorable report from it, however, carries no such weight as would be given by an endorsement from this Bureau. Furthermore, it can choose the products on which it wishes to make tests and reports.

"As has been indicated above, if this Bureau were to issue reports on products of a given kind, it would be under extreme pressure to cover not only competing products of the same kind, but others as well. In other words, as a Government agency we could not well offer a service which would be of value to one class or group of manufacturers and dealers, and refuse it to others.

"As a closing comment on this general subject, we might recall a discussion of this problem of testing consumer goods at a special session of the American Academy of Political and Social Science many years ago. At that time certain more or less competent authorities who advocated the creation of a general testing service, estimated the cost of 100 million dollars per year."

The estimate of $100 million was made in 1934, and the cost would probably be $200 million today, but this is less than one sixth of one per cent of personal expenditures for durable and non-durable goods every year!

At a Lobby conference held in 1944, on "Shall It Be Century of the Common Man or Century of Cartel Control?," Dr. Walton H. Hamilton of Yale Law School stated:

"The business unit has become the corporate state. An aggregate of separate enterprises has been organized into a political economy. If wealth must serve in massed form, it must be operated, not by owners but through representative authority. Its government cannot be of a small self-appointed group; it must be responsive to all the interests— technicians, managers, investors, laborers, consumers—who have a stake in it. And its operation must serve a larger public interest, which includes the whole economy and reaches ahead to posterity.

"Far more important than the form of an economic order is the commonwealth which it serves. We cannot depend upon any self-elected group, however noble and good, to look out for the common man."

Little similarity can be detected between such doctrines and the "New Deal."

In the summer of 1949, I made a survey of the enormous spread between prices farmers get for their products and prices consumers pay, and of farmers' costs of production, which the Lobby submitted at an open hearing of the Senate Sub-Committee on Agriculture, of which Sen. Guy M. Gillette of Iowa was Chairman, with a request his Committee make a further study and recommend legislation or Government action to protect consumers. We asked, as in all such efforts, executives of farm, labor, women's and church organizations to join in the request.

W. P. Kennedy, President the Brotherhood of Railroad Trainmen, had an editorial in his weekly *Trainmen News* favoring it, and wrote Sen. Gillette the study "is of vital importance to the welfare of our country." The Annual Session of The National Grange that fall adopted a resolution favoring it, which its able legislative counsel, Dr. J. T. Sanders, transmitted to Senator Gillette, asking to be allowed to state the Grange viewpoint. The Gillette committee and its capable Counsel, Paul Hadlick, investigated coffee, milk, bread and meat prices, but was unable to get funds, and little was done.

That June Dr. Colston E. Warne of Amherst College, Vice President of People's Lobby, President of Consumers' Union and member the Consumers' Advisory Committee to the President's Council of Economic Advisers issued the following statement through the Lobby:

"The Council of Economic Advisors has thus far been an excellent statistical agency which has periodically expressed the pious hopes of the Administration. Its recommendations have unfortunately generally been ignored by the Congress. One may applaud its work as a vast improvement over the 'blind flying' of earlier years; yet its recommendations have typically been short-range in character and it has, under the terms of the Act which created it, continued to rely fundamentally upon private enterprise to provide stability in the economy. Such reliance is not apt to provide the solution to current economic ills.

"Many drastic steps must be taken by the government if the prosperity of recent years is to be sustained. We must start with a recognition that it is the responsibility of government to keep the output of the nation at the full productive potential through the employment of long range planning, and Federal intervention, where required. If private industry falters, the government must enter the picture promptly and affirmatively, not to sustain employment as much as to sustain national income."

Dr. Broadus Mitchell, Professor of Economics at Rutgers University, President of the Lobby, published in 1948 *The Depression Decade,* a most challenging chapter of which was entitled, "War to the Rescue"—of the "New Deal," of course! With that background he presided at a conference the Lobby organized in the summer of 1949, to discuss responsibility to consumers. Economists for the Congress of Industrial Organizations, the U.S. Chamber of Commerce and the National Grange discussed the respective responsibility of the interests they represented. Wallace J. Campbell,

Washington Representative of the Cooperative League of America, asserted:

"American consumers will never secure adequate protection of their rights until they organize their purchasing power through consumer cooperatives. More than ten million American consumers are already organized in such cooperatives."

Dr. Warne put the responsibility squarely up to the Government.

As the plundering profiteers of the war expanded their huge advertising of the "American way," wasting trainloads of timber which it would take years to replace, we wrote the Forest Service in the U.S. Department of Agriculture protesting such waste, and asking action to prevent it. On September 19, 1947, Mr. Lyle F. Watts, Chief the Forest Service, which is supposed to conserve our forests, wrote us the following astounding epistle:

"The Forest Service has not made any estimate of the amount of timber for paper which is used for advertising and we are not aware of any such study having been made by others. We do not think it practical to restrict the use of paper for advertising. Our recommended program for preventing destruction and deterioration of forest resources and for increasing the production of forest products is the better way of meeting our requirements. This puts the emphasis on producing more rather than on consuming less. We have plenty of forest land in this country to grow all the timber we need. It should not be allowed to loaf."

"Waste not, want not" had gone into the discard!

That same year we urged the President to use his adequate facilities to try to stop the waste of foods by rats, amounting to 28 million tons of foodstuffs a year, and the waste of foods in garbage, which the Food Information Division of the Department of Agriculture had estimated at about one fifth of the food purchased by American house-holders. That 28 million tons wasted was fourteen times the amount of wheat we so grudgingly finally loaned to India—with about twice our population!

The Lobby conducted a running discussion with other or-ganizations over the economic efficacy of subsidies, as we ad-vocated "direct payments where needed to marginal farmers," while labor and most of the welfare organizations favored general subsidy payments for specified products, which some years ran as high as $2.5 billion. Their reasoning seemed to be that the Federal Treasury was a self-replenishing institu-tion—the dream of every profligate politician.

We consistently worked for measures to reduce costs of production and distribution of farm products, but organized labor seemed to prefer the high prices charged farmers for machinery, implements, fertilizers, etc., because these pro-duced larger profits, and seemed to justify labor's demand for continually increasing wage rates.

We asked the two Chairmen of the Senate and House Com-mittees on Interstate and Foreign Commerce to request the Interstate Commerce Commission to "appear at a Joint Hear-ing of the two Committees and state on what theory they so in-terminably raise rates, and to what extent existing legislation prevents them from protecting consumers against the un-controlled rapacity of the railroads they are supposed to con-trol," and finally in 1949, citing the fact that in the preced-ing two and a half years total rate increases the Commission had granted railroads had increased consumers' bills by nearly $4 billion, we opposed further increases until Con-gress:

"1. Vests regulation of wages and working conditions of railway employees, and regulation of freight rates, passenger fares, commutation fares, pullman rates, express rates and railway-mail pay in one Government Agency.

"2. Effectively divorces all railway executives and directors from interest in concerns from which the railroads buy supplies and equipment.

"3. Consolidates all railroads, for the benefit of everyone except those who find employment through duplication and that superlative waste of time and money called competition."

The Railwaymen's unions had the organization, money, and votes to defeat every effort at efficiency and economy on the railroads, and for efficient and coordinated transportation, including the successful fight for many years against the St. Lawrence Waterway.

Another economic fallacy was that competition was the mother of efficiency and of low prices for the benefit of consumers. A brilliant Boston lawyer, Louis Brandeis, was enthusiastic for the economic therapy of competition, and so for trust busting. Edward A. Filene, another Bostonian, was a strong advocate of mass markets, which, as he realized, meant large production and distribution units. His Boston department store is a highly profitable evidence of the worth of his views, and he defended them cogently at many Congressional Committee hearings. William Jennings Bryan was an early apostle of "trust-busting," as he preferred to crucify mankind upon a cross of costly duplicating competition rather than upon a cross of gold. Now they get it both ways!

When the Sherman Anti-Trust Law was enacted, Jackson H. Ralston at the time as for many years was Counsel for the American Federation of Labor, which had backed it strongly. He told me that he warned Sam Gompers and the AFL leaders it would be used against labor and not against industrial combines, and of course it was. The Clayton Anti-

Trust Act was a futile effort to block the natural evolution of large units, by prohibiting acquisition of stocks of one corporation by another if it would tend materially to lessen competition.

For most of the thirty-three years I worked in Washington, flaying size was a major sport of politicians, except during the two World Wars when they concentrated their fire on trying to get as big profits for the little concerns in their districts and states as the major corporations were getting out of war contracts. Most Americans are extremely anxious to get into the class they are most vigorously damning.

At the Lobby Conference early in 1944 "Shall It Be Century of the Common Man or Century of Cartel Control?" at which Prof. Walton Hamilton noted the fact cited earlier that "the business unit has become the corporate state," Maury Maverick, President Smaller War Plants Corporation, stated the view of the worshippers of the diminutive:

"The strength of this nation is not to be found in million or multi-million dollar factories, although there will be some of that kind. Rather it is to be found in the thousands of small shops and plants, where men are struggling for a vision and looking to a goal, where new ideas are developed and new methods are perfected in the toil of men who work for themselves and their loved ones."

No one knew better than Maury Maverick that a small enterprise is one which has not yet achieved the monopoly status to which its owners aspire, and which they devoutly, usually, strive to attain.

Berle and Means' masterly analysis of American industry, *The Modern Corporation,* stimulated the mania for preventing bigness in industry and finance, at the same time labor and farm organizations were rapidly increasing membership and influence!

I appeared repeatedly at hearings of Committees of both Senate and House on the several bills introduced by Senator O'Mahoney, Mr. Kefauver—while he was in the House—and others, to forbid the acquisition of the assets, as well as the stock, of another corporation. I pointed out that trade associations and similar agencies were specifically designed to do for their members what monopoly was charged with doing, but without the stigma attached to "monopoly," and quoted the statement of Hon. Wendell Berge, while he was in charge of the Anti Trust Division of the Justice Department, that even that regulator of business ethics wasn't sure just what was legal for a trade association.

I also stressed the fact the bills didn't prohibit acquisition of the assets of a firm or partnership, which partly nullified its alleged objective, and that if it were amended to include such business it could easily result in driving some plants whose production was needed for the nation's economy into closing down, after which they could probably be gobbled up by a large corporation seeking either vertical or horizontal expansion, for a song, but with no resultant benefits either to consumers or to the owners of the small concerns. Requiring businesses to have a Federal license, as provided in the O'Mahoney bill, of course would permit better supervision.

The bill as it finally became law in 1950 requires the Federal Trade Commission to certify that acquisition will not materially reduce competition, but does not ensure that any of the savings from large scale operation, competitive or otherwise, will inure to the benefit of consumers. The Lobby recommended that Congress:

"1. Decide what enterprises must be monopolies in order to be efficiently and economically operated, and devise measures to protect the consumers of the products and services thereof.

"2. Devise methods of enforcing genuine competition between enterprises it decides can best serve consumers through competition."

Neither monopolies nor little business likes this program!

It would take an unreconstructed optimist to believe that pulverizing production provides economies, or that the Trade Commission can keep adequate tabs. The present generation has forgotten the dissolution of the oil trust, which was supposed to be a Magna Charta for oil and gasoline consumers but did not restrict prices or profits or, of itself, lower prices.

When the Department of Justice in 1949 threatened to break the Atlantic and Pacific Tea Co. into seven concerns, we challenged it to prove that food and grocery chains had kept up prices to consumers, or that the course the Department recommended would in any way benefit consumers; and got a good deal of publicity on this challenge—but no reply from the Department. The matter has apparently been dropped, for the Department, since its initial call on the A & P Co. for data, has not made a move against it.

The bipartisan effort to hamstring Federal Power Commission regulation of natural gas; to give private concerns the right to exploit natural resources scores of miles out at sea off the coasts of California, Texas and Louisiana, and to vest ownership of such resources in states instead of the Federal Government, was one of the most serious threats to consumers—not yet ended. The Lobby was the first consumers' organization to oppose in 1947 the Rizley bill—which had passed the House—before a Senate Committee, after it was introduced by Senator E. H. Moore, a Republican millionaire oilman of Oklahoma. Leland Olds, as a member of the Federal Power Commission, had told the Committee it might cost consumers $200,000,000 a year in higher gas rates.

It did not pass the Senate, but Senator Robert Kerr, a Democratic millionaire oilman of Oklahoma, who was elected in 1948 to succeed Senator Moore, promptly reintroduced the bill, which was passed by Congress but was vetoed by the President. Senator Paul Douglas of Illinois successfully led the fight on the Senate floor against the bill, and urged a Presidential veto—which Congress could not over-ride.

Natural resources are both non-partisan and bi-partisan— just like their owners. The Supreme Court, in a notable decision in 1947, ruled that the Federal Government has "paramount rights" in the offshore areas. State officials of several states, including Texas, California, and Louisiana and some other oil states, tried to circumvent this decision by legislation to waive Federal rights in these areas. Their campaign was well financed, organized, and had the backing of most of the Congressional delegations from oil and natural gas states—as they usually worked together. *United States News & World Report* (May 7, 1948) stated:

"Beneath the Gulf of Mexico there may be 15,000,000,000 barrels of oil, worth at present prices $40 billion, and equal to three-fourths of present U.S. reserves. In a race to prove the theory that oil bearing formations under the land might extend out to sea, 15 companies have leased 2,500,000 acres of sea area from Louisiana and Texas at a cost of more than $25,000,000 the first year. Exploration is going on as far as 60 miles from shore, and geologists believe oil may underlie much of the Continental Shelf, which is 50 to 125 miles wide."

It warned that "international complications are a possibility," and stated "other nations could protest U.S. exploitation of what they might regard as 'international domain,' but oilmen, in race for new sources, aren't waiting for answer, expect states to win."

Judge Sam Hobbs, conservative constitutional lawyer and member of Congress from Alabama, had several times argued to Congressional Committees that the action violated international law. He couldn't mention the fact that it was as much an act of aggression as the later crossing of the 38th Parallel in Korea, with armed forces.

I had exposed the deal before the Senate Committee and in the press, and had urged peace, labor and civic organizations to do so, though few if any acted and it looked certain to pass, and in an election year a veto would have been hard to get and harder to sustain. I took all the facts to Albert S. Goss, National Master of the Grange, which has a pretty good record on conservation and public power, and asked him to try to block it. He opposed it before the Senate Committee, and also wrote a letter to all Senators stating:

"You don't often get letters from us like this, but we feel most earnestly that the Congress will make a grave mistake if it should give away the Government's oil properties as a result of the drive to pass H.R. 5992 or S. 1988.

"The issue is more far reaching than giving away government property and the enrichment of a few states at the expense of the rest. It involves both interstate and international complications of a very serious nature. If the offshore areas are given to the coastal states, hasty or head-strong action of any one of a half dozen states could involve us in serious international trouble, and the Congress would be powerless to prevent it.

"Once this bill becomes law, Congress cannot correct the error without billions of cost, and possibly not even then.

"We can see no reason for all the haste, except the desire of a few oil companies to get control of some of the nation's richest resources before the people wake up to what has happened. State ownership would certainly dissipate these invaluable strategic resources that may mean almost life or death to our nation in a possible future war."

Despite this, Congress passed the bill, but the President vetoed it and his veto wasn't overridden. It was reintroduced in the 81st and 82nd Congress, and will probably be an issue until there is national public ownership of oil, with much reduced payments to the governments of states in which located.

We can't get the century of the common man until government becomes consumer-conscious, and only a consumer-conscious people can make a government that.

CHAPTER TWELVE

Un-American Activities
Committee Swindle

ON MAY 9th, 1947, as Executive Secretary of the People's Lobby, I wrote President Truman: "Can you inform us what is the present ownership and control status of the international cartels which German nationals organized and manipulated before the recent war? Specifically, is the ownership or control, under any agreement between Britain, the United States, France and Russia, to be returned to German nationals? Do the United States, Britain, France and Russia have jurisdiction of cartels whose headquarters were located in their zone of Germany, or is there joint jurisdiction?

"If American nationals are found at the forthcoming trial of German cartelists, or by other means, to have been involved with German and other nationalists in activities and practices giving aid and comfort to the enemy, is there any direct law, or have you authority under war powers, to con-

fiscate their property for the American people, or for relief
of all victims of German action? If not, are American citizens
found guilty of the same practices as German to be punished
in any other way?"

The President referred this letter to the State Department,
and on June 12th Raymond Vernon of the International
Resources Division replied "For the Secretary of State":
"This is in reply to your letter to the President of May 9,
1947 which was referred to this office. You inquire as to the
status of German participation in international cartels and
as to measures that may be taken against American nationals
found in the forthcoming trial of German industrialists to
have given aid and comfort to the enemy.

"Laws were recently promulgated by military government
in the United States and British Zones of Germany declaring
domestic cartels to be illegal and prohibiting German participation in international cartels. These statutes are Law 56
in the United States Zone and Ordinance 78 in the British
Zone. Primary jurisdiction of all enterprises, including cartels, subject to the decartelization laws rest with the occupy-
ing power in whose zone the headquarters of the enterprise
is located, but efforts are now being made to extend the
jurisdiction of the bizonal administration in cartel matters.
Except for quadripartite action with respect to I.G. Far-
benindustrie pursuant to Control Council Law No. 9, no
arrangements exist for joint action with respect to cartels or
combines located in the French and Soviet Zones.

"There is no law or war power authorizing the confisca-
tion of property of American citizens whom United States
military tribunals in Germany at the forthcoming trial of
German industrialists may find to have been involved with
Germans in activities and practices giving aid or comfort to
the enemy. The indictment against German industrialists

and the jurisdiction of the military tribunals in Germany are based respectively on Control Council Law No. 10 which defines crimes against peace, war crimes and crimes against humanity and on Military Government Ordinance No. 7. These enactments were promulgated in Germany and apply only therein.

"The laws of this country which might conceivably be relevant to Americans implicated in the forthcoming trial include the Trading with the Enemy Act, the Sherman Antitrust Law and the sections of the Criminal Code dealing with treason. Persons who have violated these laws are subject to penalties including forfeiture of property as provided in such laws. Whether proceedings can and should be taken against American citizens who may be guilty of the practices of which Germans are now being indicted in Germany is a question which can best be answered by the Attorney General. Accordingly, we have transmitted a copy of your letter to him for further consideration."

On June 23d, Mr. John F. Sonnett, Ass't. Attorney General, wrote me: "The participation of American industrialists in foreign cartel arrangements has already been the subject of a number of anti-trust actions, and it will continue to be the purpose of this Department to prevent and punish restrictive cartel arrangements to the full extent of the law."

This didn't answer my letter to the President, so I wrote Mr. Sonnett again, and he replied July 29th: "As you know, the matters referred to in your letter of May 9, 1947 can be prosecuted only to the extent that they constitute violations of our statutes. The basic charges contained in the pending cartel indictments in Germany are not comprehended by existing legislation in the United States. To that extent, therefore, the only recourse is to Congress."

On August 5th I wrote Hon. J. Parnell Thomas, Chair-

man the House Committee on Un-American Activities, en-
closing carbon or copy of all our correspondence on the subject, with the President, State and Justice Departments:
"The People's Lobby has for some months been trying to
get the facts about the part Americans played in helping
German controlled cartels to further Germany's plans for
world domination, and what was to be done to punish such
spurious patriots, and to see that they make proper restitu-
tion to Americans and to all peoples.

"Senator Harley M. Kilgore in a 'Foreword' to Darel Mc-
Conkey's book *Out of Your Pocket—The Story of Cartels,*
says: 'In 1918, Germany was a defeated nation. Less than
twenty years later she was startlingly successful in the first
steps of a deliberate campaign to conquer the world. How
was this possible? We know the answer now. The cartel system in great measure was responsible. The German cartelists
were the real power behind the Hitler dictatorship. Their
funds and influence made possible Nazi seizure of power.'

"I enclose carbon of our letter to the President on the
status of Americans who were in cahoots with German cartelists, on May 9th, and carbon or copy of our correspondence with the State Department and the Department of
Justice on the subject since. Mr. Sonnett's letter of July
29th puts on Congress full responsibility for adequate action
to punish Americans who helped enemies of their country.
Their activities were un-American if anything ever was, and
use of forged patriotism is certainly as serious as use of forged
passports.

"These private international cartels, which can be helped
by consent decrees here, are again concocting conspiracies
against the peace and small pocketbooks of the world. We
ask that your Committee, certainly by next month, get information about American participation in cartels, and plans

for future participation, and draft legislation to compel resti-
tution by un-Americans who conspire against their country
in cartels, and also legislation to punish such un-American
activities.

"Among witnesses for your Committee we suggest: President Truman, former Chairman the Senate Committee investigating the Defense Program; Senators Harley M. Kilgore, Joseph C. O'Mahoney and Owen J. Brewster; Hon.
Wendell Berge, Hon. Thurman Arnold, Judge Homer T.
Bone, and Messrs. Howard W. Ambruster, Herman A. Ber-
man, Joseph K. Borkin and Darel McConkey. American oil,
magnesium, chemical, steel, aluminum and many other interests should also be asked to testify—if not to confess."

On August 6th, the next day, Mr. Thomas replied: "I am
in receipt of your letter of recent date, together with enclosures. I have read your communication and enclosures
with a great deal of interest and shall be glad to call this
matter to the attention of the Committee at an early date."

On October 21st, the House Committee on Un-American
Activities not having done anything about highly placed
American subversives, I wrote the Chairman again, remind-
ing him of his pledge of August 6th to take it up with the
Committee at an early date: "That was two and a half
months ago. The matter is of current vital interest, because
these same cartels threaten to imperil the success of the Marshall plan for their selfish profiteering purposes.

"Can your Committee turn from the remote threat of subversive activities in the motion picture industry to the immediate danger of international cartels, including American
industrialists, threatening the peace of the World again?"

I finally made an appeal in an open letter to Vice President Alben W. Barkley and Speaker Sam Rayburn to act,
but drew a blank—again. The contrast between the Govern-

ment's treatment of Americans who conspired with alien enemies to defeat America, and its treatment of American communists, who may have given atom bomb and other secrets to Russia while she was associated with us and suffering the most prodigious losses, does not need amplification.

Was the venality of American business interests imputed to them for righteousness, because they are potentially large campaign contributors, or because they had some secret deal with the Government, such as that which led the Germans in the First World War to refrain from attacking the plants of the French munitions monopoly?

CHAPTER THIRTEEN

The Campaign for International Controls

IN THE LATTER PART of Theodore Roosevelt's second term, at the suggestion of Gifford Pinchot, he issued an invitation to all major nations to send delegates to an international conference in Washington on the conservation of the world's natural resources, with a view to getting some sort of world plan for their extraction and distribution. Britain declined the invitation, and the plan fell through when President Taft refused to do anything about it.

President Wilson late in the first World War, in reply to the Pope's request he state the purposes for which the war was being fought, included: "To provide all peoples, large and small, participation upon fair terms in the economic opportunities of the world," and made it clear that included natural resources and other raw materials.

During that war Bernard M. Baruch, Chairman of the

War Industries Board, had major charge of the allocation of essential raw materials between America and the nations with which we were associated. Shortly after the war, I asked him whether we could have won without such international control and he admitted it was very doubtful.

"Then," I asked him, "why don't we continue such controls to facilitate reconstruction?"

"Because private owners won't permit it," he replied.

To my next question whether scrapping such controls and going back to competition wouldn't mean another world war, he said, "Probably."

At the close of the war, Mr. Baruch had urgently recommended to the President that we stockpile strategic minerals as a means of stopping future outbreaks, but nothing was done about it—then. Mr. Baruch voiced the same opinion about private owners in a report he, with his associate John M. Hancock, made February 15, 1944 on "War and Post-War Adjustment Policies": "With peace . . . each has the right to make what he pleases. Governmental direction and aid disappear. The markets become free, and each individual is dependent upon his vision, his courage, his resourcefulness and his energy. . . . The American system has outproduced the world. It is easier to convert from peace to war, than from war to peace. With the coming of war, a sort of totalitarianism is asserted."

Mr. Baruch's and Mr. Hancock's statement ignores the existence of protective tariffs, "basing points," government subsidies, "parity prices," government loans and government tax rebates, and unemployment and old age benefits!

Mr. Baruch's admission in 1921 led me on December 5th that year, as Managing Director of the Farmers National Council, to write President Harding the following program asking him to submit it to the Conference on the Limitation of Armaments:

"Arrangements must be made to pool the natural resources of the world—coal, iron, copper, oil, etc.—so that these will all be accessible and available to all nations, very particularly to Japan, upon fair terms. We must create an International Investment Board, representing the nations of the world, to control concessions and special privileges granted to any national of a foreign country by any other nation, in order to prevent the concession land-grabbing and financial imperialism which has been such a continuing cause of war, and which will continue to be a cause of war." Nothing came of this.

In 1928 Ludwell Denny, then as now associated with the Scripps-Howard papers, published his masterly book, "We Fight for Oil," in which he poignantly said: "Modern international power is economic. The nation which controls oil and other raw materials, foreign markets and credits will rule the world." He sharpened the issue in his statement: "Anglo-American strife over foreign resources (of oil) has become a major factor in international affairs. The British perhaps have been more militant, because their need has been until now so much greater than ours. But in motive and in method there is little difference between the contending forces." We gave wide publicity to the facts and findings of this book.

After World War One Winston Churchill, as Lord of the Admiralty, started to convert the British Navy from coal to oil, which profoundly affected Britain's domestic and foreign policies.

Toward the expiration of President Coolidge's second term, after he had the caution not to choose to run, I asked Gifford Pinchot if he would draft an appeal to the President to call an international conference on the conservation and equitable distribution of the world's natural resources, to be signed by leaders in labor, farm, church and civic organizations. He complied and prepared a statesmanlike presentation, which was signed by such leaders, including Wm. Green, President of the American Federation of Labor (the Congress of Industrial Organizations had not then been organized), John L. Lewis, President the United Mine Workers, other labor leaders, farmer spokesmen, and church leaders. This was given to President Hoover shortly after his inauguration, but he ignored it entirely—though it was well publicized.

Such a conference would certainly have done more for the peace of the world than the "good-will" trip which Mr. Hoover made to South American countries on a huge U.S. battleship, labeled a peace mission!

The Hoover Administration was too much concerned with prospecting for the elusive prosperity around the corner; the first Roosevelt term with trying to put some semblance of prosperity around the corner, with complete disregard of the world situation; and the second Roosevelt term with covering up on the fact the prosperity of the first term was phony —to permit much attention to international organization.

Despite the brave bluff words of Hoover and Roosevelt, from 1929 to 1940 America was chiefly concerned with extricating herself from the world disorganization we had done so much to foster. It is better politics, in a nation whose operating God is hypocrisy, to create an aggressor and then identify and threaten to quarantine him, than to put your own house in order and pluck out the beam that is in your own eye so you can see the mote that is in your brother's. Plucking out our own beam is not, however, the way to get three or four terms in the White House.

During those twelve years, we did our pamphleteering against imperialism—"American Capitalism Abroad," noted earlier—held several conferences on the subject in Washington; and I discussed the issue and the need for international controls and co-operation in most of the hundreds of meetings, large and small, in my speaking trips from Boston to Seattle and Los Angeles. I found students in both state and private institutions keenly interested; a good many sensed ahead, by the late thirties, that they might have to walk the military plank and even make the supreme sacrifice for the supreme stupidity of a Government which was trying to live too much by itself, and even then had the economic delirium tremens implicit in the term "The American Century."

In the summer of 1929 I presented the plan urged by the Pinchot group to the Anti-Imperialist Conference in Frankfort-on-the-Main, mentioned earlier; to members of the Secretariat of the League of Nations at Geneva; and to the Executive Committee of the Second International (Socialist) meeting at Zurich. All admitted the merits, few expected action. At Zurich the Belgian representative asked whether I remembered the Belgian Congo, and the Socialist leader from Holland, if I realized what Indonesian resources meant to his country!

In the mid thirties we got a member of the House of Representatives to introduce for us a bill for public ownership of coal, oil, water-power and gas, which was referred to the House Committee on Ways and Means. This was an approach to the "Giant Power System" which Gifford Pinchot had long and ably advocated, but we were again unable to get any farm, labor, church, civic or peace organization to join us in requesting a hearing, and it died in several Congresses without any burial services—hearings.

Unfortunately we couldn't get Secretary of the Interior

Harold L. Ickes to back even a hearing, though early in the New Deal two of the really progressive lawyers in the Department asked our help in drafting a bill for public ownership of coal, but they were promptly dissuaded or squelched by the invisible government which is an integral part of private monopoly. I refrain from giving their names, lest their usefulness be impaired by the smear of "subversive."

Pearl Harbor, and the use by the Japanese of the implements of aggression which we had so lavishly furnished them, put a temporary quietus on our efforts to get some form of international control. In late 1942, however, when the British Labor Party looked ahead to the defeat of the Triple Axis, and boldly and baldly declared for international control of the production and distribution of natural resources, particularly oil, and of commerce and currency, and international allocation of markets, we renewed our efforts for a program that would give some hope that World War Two would not be merely a breeder of World War Three.

Sir Stafford Cripps, at the time Lord Privy Seal, about the same time stated: "One thing is sure—that the United Nations must, at the end of the war, undertake the international regulation of the production and distribution of essential raw materials, both in the interest of immediate rehabilitation of the devastated countries, as well as with a view to attaining that steadily rising standard of living throughout the world which is one of our objectives."

We accepted the Labor Party's view that no such controls or cooperation were practical without Government ownership of natural resources and monopolies, and an over all Government plan for the economy.

We got a lot of publicity on our program, and the opposition got vocal and vociferous.

In March 1942 the Petroleum Administration for War

had appointed a "Foreign Operations Committee," composed of thirteen representatives of big American oil companies, and of two British oil companies—the Anglo-Iranian Oil Co. Ltd., and the Asiatic Petroleum Corporation.

In the summer of 1943 Dr. C. K. Leith, of Wisconsin University, specialist on minerals in the War Production Board, enunciated a new "peace" proposal: "The firm control of raw materials, by an international policing body for the enforcement of peace." He outlined the plan in June 1943: "That the international flow of minerals be controlled by a group of nations, which may be formed at the end of the war for the purpose not only of equitable distribution (of minerals) for legitimate needs, but of policing the world and keeping peace." He stated: "The English-speaking people alone control three-quarters of the world's minerals, politically and commercially. Theirs is the principal responsibility for anything that may be done with raw materials in the interest of peace," and he suggested the United Nations "withhold from the Axis powers or any other recalcitrant nations the supplies necessary to build up armaments to a scale which would menace the peace of the world, while at the same time allowing all nations enough for peace-time needs."

A "recalcitrant" nation has come to mean one which doesn't bow the knee to the system of private profits, and challenges the concept of "The American Century"—but Dr. Leith's plan had been accepted by the real rulers of America and their elected Government stooges.

On October 7, 1943, Charles E. Wilson, Acting Chairman the War Production Board, submitted to the Attorney General "Petroleum Directive 70 of the Petroleum Administration for War," approved by Secretary Ickes, giving the major oil companies full power to arrange for facilities, materials and supplies of petroleum, in cases requiring immediate action, "without the approval of the Director." On December 16, 1943 this "Foreign Operations Committee" issued a report, "A Foreign Oil Policy for the United States," which asserted: "Oil development can best be handled by private enterprise." Consistent with its self-interest, it stated: "In the period of transition from war to peace, questions will arise as to the disposition of oil facilities abroad which the Government of the United States has acquired in the course of the war. In general such facilities should be disposed of to private enterprise.

"The American petroleum industry should be admitted more fully into the policy councils of the Government of the United States, and its ideas and experience should be availed of in a consultative capacity in all policies and measures affecting the future status of foreign oil operations."

It is also urged that an "International Oil Compact" be negotiated to provide "efficient and orderly development of the world's oil resources," and "prudent conservation" thereof; "equitable distribution of oil to the peoples of all nations," and "avoidance of national restrictions imposed as artificial aids to the production of synthetic or substitute products." There was not to be any escape from profiteering oil barons!

On January 16, 1944, the Petroleum Industry War Council announced it had established a committee composed of oil industry executives "to formulate a national government oil policy for recommendation to the government, including both foreign and domestic phases of a long-range petroleum program." Just a month later the Senate (Truman) Committee Investigating the National Defense Program, like oiled seals, issued a report of its sub-committee on petroleum matters overseas, showing that companies controlled by United States nationals produced about 84.2% of the world's production.

As to the future, the Committee held: "The acquisition of foreign oil rights has become affected with a strong national interest. To secure possession of such rights would be a determining factor in preventing future wars, for aggressive nations will hesitate to attack us if they know that we have the petroleum, as well as the other weapons, with which to defend ourselves. It is therefore necessary for the United States to evolve a detailed policy for the exploration and development of foreign oil resources."

It listed four "approaches to our solution": continuing the policy of relying upon private grabbing, "with Government assistance limited to that available through normal diplomatic channels"; "full diplomatic backing for American enterprise in exploring and developing foreign petroleum reserves," and "the third and fourth alternatives are for the Government to participate in the ownership of the concessions or to take over the sole ownership of certain foreign oil reserves."

The Truman Committee commented: "Complete Government ownership of foreign oil concessions would presuppose a radical change in our economic system." The Committee refused to consider, even, international controls such as the British Labor Party advocated and People's Lobby had urged upon it.

Michael Straight, writing in the *New Republic* early in 1942, under the caption "Standard Oil-Axis Ally," stated: "At heart we all know that public ownership alone can free our strength," and an editorial entitled "Standard Oil and the War," called upon Nelson Rockefeller, Co-ordinator of Inter-American Affairs, to make "a clear public statement disavowing the actions of his company," because "without such a statement, his reputation and that of his good neighbor organization will suffer with most Latin Americans." Mr. Rockefeller remained mum and millionaire!

The *Nation,* and *Christian Century,* and a few other religious papers, exposed the racket, and a few of the daily press, but hot war, like cold, congeals the courage of most people.

Early in 1944 Harold L. Ickes, Secretary of the Interior and Petroleum Administrator, stated: "Tell me the sort of agreement that the United Nations will reach with respect to the world's petroleum resources when the war is over, and I will undertake to analyze the durability of the peace that is to come." While Mr. Ickes was Petroleum Administrator, the oil interests not only looted the Government mercilessly but dug themselves in all over the world.

At the Lobby's conference in April 1944 James B. Carey, Secretary-Treasurer the Congress of Industrial Organizations, discussing "Labor's Post-War Program," said: "International and national stability are interdependent. Cooperation between nations is an essential part of present-day economics and politics." The CIO program, he said, includes: "A federal planning agency to see that national resources are used intelligently, for the benefit of all the people." This was ignored in the CIO's scramble to get a bigger cut of profits for its dues-paying members, and its fight to keep the American Federation of Labor from raiding its unions.

The A.F. of L. was too engrossed in holding its membership and getting more fool's gold—slowly rising wage rates in a fast moving inflation—to concern itself with basic issues.

In March 1946, when an impasse in Iran threatened, we wrote Trygve Lie, Secretary-General the United Nations Organization, asking that when this issue was brought before the Council, the Governments of the United States, Britain and Russia be asked to make public the terms of their existing and sought oil concessions in Iran. The letter was not acknowledged, nor the request made!

In June 1947 I appeared before the Senate Committee on Foreign Relations on the Anglo-American Oil Agreement, which Britain had approved, and which provided for joint action by the two nations on exploitation of the world's oil resources, and convening an international conference of oil producing and oil consuming countries, on control of the industry, multilaterally. I stated: "Until our Government owns the oil resources of America it will, of course, be impossible to have a world plan for oil, and this Committee would distinguish itself above all previous performance by noting that fact, and urging the Government own the oil instead of the oil interests owning the Government.

"An agreement to control the development of the oil resources of the world, allocate the supply, and determine the price thereof, should be made by the Economic and Social Council of the United Nations, or by some agency thereof, and approved by the United Nations."

We wrote Trygve Lie at the United Nations, urging it act, but with no success, nor did a single major peace, farm, labor, church or civic organization back the plea.

About the same time the International Cooperative Alliance, a consultant of the Economic and Social Council of the United Nations, proposed to the Council that a conference of the sovereign states of the Middle East be convened and asked to delegate to the United Nations Petroleum Commission responsibility "to see that oil concessionaires in the Middle Eastern states operate in the general public interest, plan and enforce oil conservation measures," and to see that all purchasers of oil, large and small, government and non-government, including cooperatives, "can buy oil on a basis of equality and in adequate quantities." It also asked this U.N. Commission "serve as a tribunal to adjudicate any oil disputes that might arise," since there was not at the time (or since) any such tribunal. This was to be an administrative agency, not a judicial one like the International Court of Justice at the Hague.

In August 1947, the Economic and Social Council voted 8 to 2 merely to "take note" of this proposal, deciding that such control was not necessary at that time. "Our" Government of course opposed it, and Britain, scared by its economic plight, joined us. Howard A. Cowden, President the Consumers Cooperative Association, prime mover for the Commission, commented on the Council's action: *"The acid test of United Nations is whether or not it can regulate the great economic empires, such as the big oil companies, in the public interest."*

It is obvious that the United Nations, made up of national governments, cannot do this unless those governments regulate such empires within their jurisdiction, and America doesn't, while Britain does only partially yet.

After attending the fiftieth reunion of my class at Grinnell College (Iowa) in 1948, I sat in on a conference on international problems sponsored by the college, at which a galaxy of speakers including Dorothy Thompson, Norman Thomas, Clarence Streit and Ely Culbertson advocated an international police force. The Chairman at the first meeting tried to rush through a resolution favoring this, but it was blocked, though passed in modified form later, evidence the middle west doesn't stampede as easily as in the old days!

During the conference attended by about 150 delegates chiefly from civic and college organizations of the state, I introduced and discussed a resolution to the effect the conference favored such government control of the oil industry in America as would facilitate the international controls essential to maintain the peace—which was approved by about one third of the audience. All the celebrated speakers at the conference seemed scared of controls.

The decision of the United States Supreme Court upholding the paramount interest of the Federal Government in submerged off-shore oil and other natural resources, and the efforts of the oil interests to circumvent this decision by legislation, show the vital importance of the ownership and control of oil in the nation's domestic and foreign policies.

Roger W. Babson does not need to be acquitted of the charge of being a radical. In one of his syndicated articles published in February 1951, he wrote:

"People who own and develop oil land are entitled to receive fair compensation for their risk and expenses; but God will not forgive the hogging of this precious oil against the welfare of mankind. It truly seems as if the entire world is crazy not to insist now on a fair distribution of this oil to all nations, including Russia. For not leading such a movement, it seems as if the United Nations is the 'international insane asylum' of our world. . . .

"Until every nation—including Russia and China—has a fair quantity of oil, we must expect another world war. As God 'sends His rain on the just and unjust,' so the United Nations should send the oil of Iran to every nation, instead of cowardly sitting by and making speeches.

"The United Nations should stop arguing over technicalities and calling each other names like silly children. The delegates should realize that God gave the world the great oil fields. The delegates should insist that Iran shall have a just recompense and not be scared by bribes, threats or intrigue, whether by England, Russia or the United States.

"The United Nations should further insist on a fair distribution of this oil and have all nations recognize that they need not resort to war to keep from being shut off from these God given resources. This is an illustration of what the United Nations should plan and fight for. Have we 'Christian' nations forgotten the four freedoms, to which Churchill and Roosevelt agreed, when World War II was going against them?"

In an April 1951 column, he warned: "Our hope and safety lie not with more bombers, more ships and more ground troops, but in assuring the world of the four freedoms which we offered them nearly 10 years ago."

The alternative to international controls and organization —with Russia if possible, without her if necessary—is international disaster and chaos, People's Lobby always held; and, as this record shows, we worked for such controls consistently.

CHAPTER FOURTEEN

Reflections on a Half Century's Work

THE READER who has gotten this far will, I hope, indulge me in a few reflections, based upon rather wide observation of how political democracy works in the capital of the richest and, temporarily at least, the most powerful nation in the world—which has not yet accepted the mandate: "Let him among you who would be greatest, be the servant of you all."

Americans are today predominantly acquisitive, and sub-consciously at least—as evidenced by the relatively slow growth of the cooperative movement compared with Britain and the Scandinavian countries—extreme individualists. Morality is adjustment to environment, and while such in-dividualism was inevitable in opening up a continent it is fatal when nearly all the good free land has been in private, if not speculative, ownership for many years.

My ground for stating in the Foreword that the three great bulwarks of reaction in America today are organized religion,

organized labor and organized farmers is that they have an
overwhelming majority of the votes; own an overwhelming
proportion of the wealth of the nation; and receive an overwhelming share of the disposable national income. They
have no alibi for permitting exploitation and injustice to continue, particularly since their own press, though chiefly
weekly, semi-weekly and monthly, has a circulation equal to
that of the metropolitan press.

The total membership of religious bodies in 1949 was
nearly 82,000,000. The total income of trade unions runs
from $550 million to $575 million a year, which is just about
two thirds of the *capital* of the three largest Foundations—
Ford, Rockefeller and Carnegie. The net income of farmers
in 1950 was nearly $19 billion, though about a seventh of
them usually get around half of the total farm income. The
assessed value of farm real estate in 1950 was over $48 billion.

As I have mentioned in connection with various social
ownership proposals of People's Lobby, we have been unable
to get backing for specific measures by major church, labor
and farm organizations, though various labor unions and
small church and farm groups have approved some social
ownership. Public power has been widely approved. The program we urged, with the exception of heavier taxation of
land values, is much like that of the British Labor Party and
of the moderate Socialist Parties of Europe.

In March 1942 the Commission on a Just and Durable
Peace of the Federal Council of Churches blue printed a post-
war peace organization, in which it stated: "We believe that
economic security is no less essential than political security
to a just and durable peace . . . Nor must it be forgotten that
refusal to assent to needed change may be as immoral as the
attempt by violent means to force such change . . . We believe that a new ordering of economic life is both imminent

and imperative, and that it will come either through voluntary co-operation within the framework of democracy, or through explosive political revolution . . . We recognize the need of experimentation with various forms of ownership and control, private, cooperative and public."

Both labor and most churches backed the Marshall Plan, as People's Lobby did, after assurance from our Government that substantially the terms laid down by this Federal Council Commission would be complied with. Within a short time however it was obvious the purpose of the Marshall Plan administration was to entrench reaction in all the countries included, as we did in Germany and Japan.

A few labor leaders, notably Walter Reuther, denounced our betrayal in Europe, but most of them, particularly stooges of the Vatican in both the AFL and the CIO, were much more concerned with denouncing communists and communism. Church organizations here seldom voiced protest against the reaction of administrators of the Marshall plan and the corrupt or utterly inefficient administration of our zone in Germany, where we have put Naziism back in the saddle, as we re-instated Fascism in Italy, and confirmed it in Spain. The support church and labor gave to the Truman Doctrine in Greece and Turkey was a supreme tragedy, as that Doctrine will make us hated there, and by all real democrats, for a long time.

While Bishop Francis J. McConnell was presiding as President, at one of the Lobby's Annual Meetings I remarked that I envied his patience in trying to Christianize the church. "Oh I gave that up long ago" he replied. I know he and a small group of church leaders in various branches of the church keep up the good fight, but the church's chief function in America is to play the game of exploiters by harping on personal salvation and extolling the economic status quo.

America's experience since the Great Depression gives too much point to the observation that all you have to do to understand dictatorships is to study democracies. Since the overdue stock market collapse of 1929, we have adopted most of the policies which were important factors in producing Hitler in Germany, and most church, farm and labor organizations have backed these policies.

During World War Two most churches were able to pay off their mortgages, so the Prince of Peace at the conclusion of that repudiation of His teachings could make a new start in edifices unencumbered by mortgages and with their governing bodies often holding a considerable block of Government "victory" bonds.

As a realist, however, the Prince of Peace could not fail to observe that the only change in belligerency in America was in temperature and in enemies. America shifted from a hot to a cold war, while a large and highly vocal part of His well heeled followers scorned every practical approach to peace and called for a crusade against "atheist" Russia and "communist" China, though we couldn't find adequate words, during the war, to express our appreciation for their help against our seasonal enemies.

In 1903, and again in 1907 and 1908, I spent a good deal of time in Germany. Bismarck had launched the social security program, as an essential in trying to achieve Deutschland über Alles. That involved giving a little higher standard of living and better sense of security to the masses of the German people, while the Kaiser challenged the British in North Africa, and "Britannia Rules the Waves." A few years later, I spent a month from the middle of December 1912 in London, while Lloyd George was campaigning for his social security and socialized medicine programs. Lloyd George was enough of a realist to know the clash with Germany was inevitable, and the British like the German Government must give tangible evidence of its solicitude for the masses of its people to hold them in line for the struggle.

I had advocated social insurance—health and employment —for two and a half decades before President Franklin Roosevelt did; but as part of a socialized economy, not as a substitute for such an economy.

In 1934, Senator Robert F. Wagner asked me whether I thought the "New Deal" had gone far enough to the Left. I assured him it hadn't gone to the Left at all, but was much slicker than the Republican Party in saving the Right while throwing a few crumbs to the masses to hold their votes. The Senator criticized the President for not pressing at that time for a full "social security" program. Roosevelt was shrewder however and wanted the war clouds, then only as big as a man's hand, to get bigger and blacker as an argument, open or implied, for his role as world stabilizer!

A "welfare" state that isn't a socialized state—whether through cooperative or public ownership—is almost certain to be a warfare state, as the record of Britain and Germany showed.

Our experience has pointed up the issue whether a people will break with tradition by making things easier for them, or by being forced by brutal compulsion to be logical and therefore radical.

Fearing that the inevitable slide in the fictitious prosperity of the "New Deal" would bring stark reaction here, our Board arranged a dinner in Washington to see if we could get backing for a Senate Committee on Civil Rights. Several Senators including Robert M. La Follette, Jr., and members of the House of Representatives, and representatives of the National Grange, Farm Bureau, National Farmers' Union, CIO and AFL, and of three great church central bodies—the Federal Council of Churches, National Catholic Welfare Council, and Central Conference of American Rabbis attended.

Senator La Follette agreed to introduce a Senate Resolution creating such a Commission, which with the open support of these church bodies, and no one else, was "kissed" through the Senate; and the Senate Committee on Civil Rights formally created, with an adequate appropriation for its work. From the very beginning, it centered its efforts under Sen. LaFollette Chairman, and Elbert D. Thomas, Democrat of Utah, Vice Chairman, on investigating violations of the right of wage earners to organize, legally sanctioned by the famous Section 7-a of the National Industrial Recovery Act. It gave little attention to other violations of civil rights, despite frequent requests to do so.

Membership in labor unions, both craft in the AFL and mass industries in the CIO, grew rapidly; but labor's interest in general economic issues waned. Under the aegis of this Section 7a and the Senate Civil Liberties Committee, great numbers of workers—around 16,000,000 at the peak—were organized to compete more nearly on a parity with owners, for a larger cut of profits—regardless of the masses of unorganized consumers. A large part of the success of this drive was due to the cooperation of those who would now be stigmatized as "fellow travelers."

It is supreme irony that there is today more communism in both AFL and CIO unions where there are equal pay rates for the alert and the lazy, than in all Russia—whose critics charge she has greater earned income disparity than America —and that the inflationary policies of organized labor (and organized farmers) here will overthrow the government long before any theoretical use of force and violence by the Communist Party could possibly do so.

As a result organized labor, with its leaders trying to get salaries well up in five figures, and huge expense accounts, has become one of the most reactionary forces in America; and much of it is more concerned with denouncing the commies than with constructive domestic or foreign policies. A labor party would have short shrift in America today; an anti-labor-excesses party would have a wide appeal.

The dominant ambition of America's rulers today is that which the Kaiser and Hitler had, and Russia has now as strongly as our own rulers: world control.

The major tragedy of the McCarthys, McCarrans, Spellmans and Henry Luces is not their blatant dishonesty, but their supernatural stupidity. They are probably worth our entire stock of atom bombs, and a hundred well equipped divisions, to Stalin; because by their Machiavellian machinations they have turned the Congress of the United States into Stalin's greatest asset.

If Russia approved the crossing of the 38th Parallel in Korea, it was as stupid as opposing an election in North Korea while it was being held under United Nations auspices in the Southern part. Russia should have learned that all that is necessary to make the United States, or any nation, disliked by the common people of a country is to have her try to run the country. She might even have anticipated the report of the United Nations, in the latter part of August 1951, that despite the billions of dollars we poured into Marshall Plan countries to raise production there, production in Eastern European countries has increased more rapidly since the war than in those we helped!

Russia has two important advantages in the race for supremacy, over the "free nations," particularly the United States, Britain, France, Belgium and Holland:

1st. The masses of the Russian people, and of the peoples in most of her satellite nations, except Czechoslovakia, have had a pretty low standard of living which can be fairly easily increased slowly, while our armament program, world aid, and Atlantic Pact are certain to lower or retard the potential improvement in the standard of living of the masses of most, if not all, of the "free nations."

2nd. Russia's limited imperialism gives her the lure of novelty in the underdeveloped nations she seeks to control, over Britain, on whose possessions the sun never used to set; over the United States, on whose investments the sun never sets; over France, now spending more to suppress freedom in Indo-China than she gets from us under the Marshall Plan; over Holland, which barely escaped disaster in Indonesia; and over Belgium, in whose Congo possessions the natives returned thanks to God when Germany overran Belgium in World War One!

Russia has two special advantages over America:

1st. Her promises, whatever her performances, are post-dated; while we are supposed to transplant our marvellous efficiency in production—which no informed person will deny—and have it going almost full tilt, instanter. It can't be done.

2nd. While our "know-how" in production is superlative our "know-what-to-do" with our "know-how" trails far behind Russia's.

William Benton, (later U.S. Senator) while Assistant Secretary of State in charge of the Voice of America, told a conference of the Associated Church Press in April 1946: "Today it devolves upon your Government to supplement the activities of foreign missions, and of *commercial agencies* and other groups." One need only contrast the effect on back-ward peoples of the announcement our "Government" was prepared to supplement our hated "commercial agencies," with the effect of the mass youth Rally in East Berlin in August 1951!

America the Beautiful seems destined to be in for a beautiful disillusionment. In a third of a century we have run the gamut of life from denunciation of scarcity, to Government subsidy of farm products scarcity, to buy the votes of farm producers, and Government subsidies to consumers of farm products, so they could buy the subsidized scarce crops, and called it "Political Democracy Triumphant."

American farmers have proved themselves highly capable, and by their anarchistic use of the soil have ruined, though not irreparably, at least a quarter of the arable land of the nation, making it the prey of both flood and drought. American labor has decided not to try to beat 'em but to join 'em, and to make common cause with profiteering owners in casting their burden on unorganized consumers. American "entrepeneurs," by acts of Congress and state Legislatures, have grabbed most of the nation's water power and other natural resources, so now we must ransack if not annex the world to make good the depletion of scarce minerals.

We shall doubtless soon have (if we haven't already) an army, air or naval base in reasonable juxtaposition to every major source throughout the world of minerals and other material needed to make ourselves as feared as we would like to be loved, by all the nations (nearly) of the world, in United Nations assembled.

Super-entrepeneurs who got hold of the nation's natural gas have wasted many trillions of cubic feet, but having heard of Maynard Keynes' and Alvin Hansen's "compensatory economy" got themselves elected, as legally as ever, to the United States Senate, which is not only a sanctuary for poltroons, but permits even members whose tongues are hung on ball bearings to talk themselves, as well as their few auditors, into a state of impotent coma.

Fortunately, though the Senate could, until recently, be described as a place where women cease from troubling and the wicked are at rest, the lady from Maine—and may her tribe increase—has by political parthogenesis summoned her many fellow conscientious objectors in that body to a keener sense of public duty.

America has reached not only a parting, but a semi-permanent if not permanent parting of the ways. She can't "choose," in the sense Calvin Coolidge did choose what to do, because conditions in the world she ignored too long narrow her choice. Today only huge government expenditures prevent a collapse of our economy, because they are paid for, not by higgling of the market, but to some extent by distribution of the national income based upon ability to pay, and benefits received from Government.

World planning, not world bossing by any one or even two nations, is the alternative to world chaos. National sovereignty is still a virulent bane, but progress can be made in time, to joint sovereignties. No child was ever born ten years of age, nor can a world government be summoned into existence overnight. It must be a gradual growth.

World organization, or planning, postulates a large degree of national planning, particularly in the major nations, since no international authority, whether it be a working union of established governments or an international agency elected by "citizens of the world," can effectively operate enterprises not subject to national control—in the present state of the world. It is pre-eminently important that national cultural autonomy be preserved, to augment the world's cultural life.

We Americans will find it hard to develop self-discipline, but self-discipline, until the state "withers away" is for us the alternative to imposed discipline.

As of 1951, the military have achieved a dangerous dominance in America not because of any inherent viciousness but because of the vacuum in our economy. The day Ogden L. Mills' appointment in the depth of the depression, as Secretary of the Treasury, was announced, I met him in the Senate Office Building where he was being congratulated, but I told him he had my sympathy. "Why?", he asked, astounded; and I told him because we had about 20,000,000 too many people for the way we let our economy operate. We figured out the surplus workers—for factory, mine, trade and transportation, and their dependents, and he admitted he didn't know what to do about it. In 1950, after the world's most extensive and expensive salvage operation for "private enterprise," America still had two or three million too many potential workers for a peace economy, and about that many too few workers for a full war economy of waste.

Reliance upon military action to remedy that situation, has been proved futile twice in the past generation. A third try could easily be fatal to us—not to the world. The release of atomic energy has not only obliterated space, wiped out national boundaries, and challenged the system of private profit—it has determined the time within which America must become consumer—and therefore cooperative and so-cial—minded.

Index of Names